AEROFILMS G

The
South Downs
Way

John Godfrey

IAN ALLAN
Publishing

THE
SOUTH DOWNS
WAY

Based on an original idea by Richard Cox
of Aerofilms

Designer: Michael D. Stride
Series Editor: Rebecca King

The publishers gratefully acknowledge the
following for the use of photographs. AA
Photo Library: pages 4, 6, 24, 25, 46, 47, 70,
71, 90, 91, 116, 117; Nature Photographers
Ltd: pages 104, 105.

First published 1992

ISBN 0 7110 2042 6

Published by Ian Allan Ltd, Shepperton, Surrey;
and printed by Ian Allan Printing Ltd at their works
at Coombelands in Runnymede, England

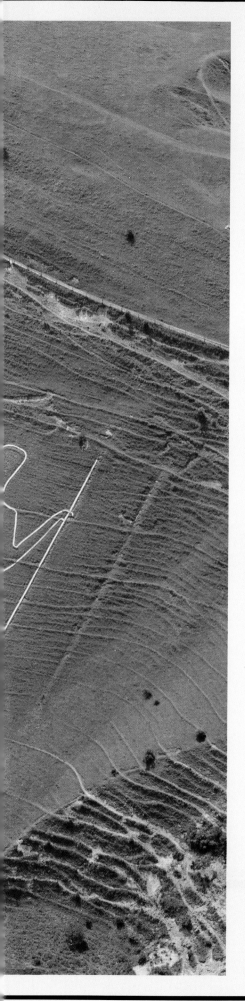

Contents

Following the Route   4-5
Practical Information   6-7
Introduction to the   8-9
South Downs Way
Index   130-131
Useful Organisations   132

THE ROUTE

Eastbourne to Alfriston   10
(FOOTPATH VIA THE SEVEN SISTERS)
Eastbourne to Alfriston   26
(BRIDLEWAY VIA JEVINGTON)
Alfriston to Lewes   32
Lewes to Devil's Dyke   48
Devil's Dyke to Washington   58
Washington to Arundel   72
Arundel to Cocking   80
Cocking to Butser   92
Butser to Exton   106
Exton to Winchester   118

FEATURES

The Coast   24-25
Castles and Fortifications   46-47
Country Houses   70-71
Churches and Cathedrals   90-91
Wildlife   104-105
Art, Music and Literature   116-117

Other titles in this series:
The South Devon Coast Path
The Cotswold Way

Following

The Countryside Commission's long-distance route symbol is an acorn and by and large waymarking along the South Downs Way in East and West Sussex is

VERTICAL PHOTO-MAPS

Every step of the Way is plotted on vertical photographs using a scale of 1:10,000 (0.6 miles:3.9ins, 1km:10cm).

COMPASS POINT

Every photo-map is accompanied by a compass point for ease of orientation.

ROUTE DIRECTIONS

These numbered route directions correspond to the numbers shown in yellow on the photo-maps. Sometimes alternative paths or optional diversions are given.

OBLIQUE PHOTOGRAPHS

These photographs bring a new perspective to the landscape and its buildings. All the subjects chosen can either be seen from, lie on, or are within easy reach of the Way.

SCALE FOR PHOTO-MAPS

The scale-bar represents a distance of 0.310 miles (0.5km).

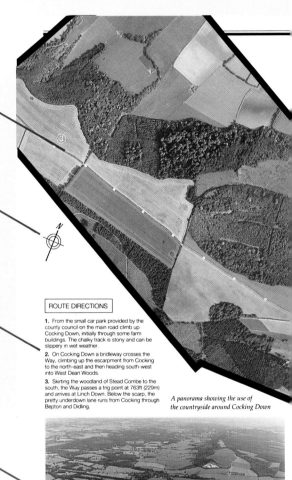

ROUTE DIRECTIONS

1. From the small car park provided by the county council on the main road climb up Cocking Down, initially through some farm buildings. The chalky track is stony and can be slippery in wet weather.

2. On Cocking Down a bridleway crosses the Way, climbing up the escarpment from Cocking to the north-east and then heading south-west into West Dean Woods.

3. Skirting the woodland of Stead Combe to the south, the Way passes a trig point at 763ft (229m) and arrives at Linch Down. Below the scarp, the pretty underdown lane runs from Cocking through Bepton and Didling.

A panorama showing the use of the countryside around Cocking Down

92

The vertical photography used in the photo-maps is taken from an average height above sea level. This means that the scale of the photography will alter slightly as the contours of the ground vary. The photo-maps are constructed by piecing together a series of photographs to make each page. They are intended to give a

he Route

excellent; signing in Hampshire is less good. The acorn symbol may be found on indicator plinths or wooden signposts, or it may be stamped on a post or stile.

Cocking to Butser
12 miles (19km)

This is a fine day's walk in some of the best scenery of the West Sussex downland, with views north over the Rother valley to Black Down and south to Chichester and the sea. There are particularly good, open views north from Harting Down, which is about half way, and the walk concludes at Queen Elizabeth country park on the A3 south of Petersfield and in the shadow of Butser Hill, at 900ft (270m) the highest point on the South Downs. Once again, there are few opportunities for refreshment *en route*, although there is a welcome café at Queen Elizabeth country park at the end of the day.

COCKING DOWN

TO THE SOUTH of the scarp lies the West Dean Estate, formerly owned by Edward James, the eccentric millionaire and art connoisseur who established and endowed the Edward James Foundation. The Foundation runs West Dean House as a college providing a range of courses in arts and crafts, and the gardens are open to the public.

The estate is also run by the Foundation, who for many years have encouraged interest in the conservation of the 6,000 acres of landscape for which they are responsible. Sympathetic farming practices have been combined with support for the establishment of Kingley Vale National Nature Reserve (north-west of Chichester), the Weald and Downland Open Air Museum (see page 89) and the recording and monitoring of the archaeology and ecology of the estate.

93

SECTIONS OF THE WAY
The route from Eastbourne to Winchester has been divided into sections that can comfortably be walked in a day. Each of these sections opens with an introduction and the distance involved is given.

SYMBOLS
The following symbols appear on the photo-maps for information and to help the walker get his bearings.

![railway]	Railway station
![viewpoint]	Viewpoint
★	Place of interest
![pub]	Pub or hotel
P	Car park
![church]	Church

GENERAL TEXT
Places to visit, points of specific interest and information relevant to that particular stretch of the route accompanies every photo-map. Tourist Boards (see page 132) will supply opening times to places to visit, and it is always advisable to check details in advance of a visit to avoid disappointment. Generally, opening times between October and Easter are very limited.

pictorial representation of the ground and strict accuracy of scale throughout cannot be guaranteed. There may also be a mismatch in areas of extreme relief – ie where the land is steepest. These problems have been kept to a minimum, in particular close to the main route of the walk.

Practical Information

ACCOMMODATION AND TRANSPORT

LOCAL PEOPLE may enjoy the South Downs Way by devising circular walks which include part of the route or by walking sections of it and returning to the starting point by public transport or, in the more remote areas, by using two cars.

Visitors may choose to do something similar, perhaps basing themselves at a convenient centre, or they may decide to tackle the whole or part of the route, arranging overnight accommodation as they go. For the first group, there is a wide choice of accommodation available in hotels, pubs, private houses and youth hostels and the local Tourist Information Centre will be pleased to help. For the traveller looking for accommodation *en route*, the choice is less wide. However, the Way is rarely far from a village or town and there is a particularly good network of youth hostels between the River Adur and Beachy Head. Camping *sauvage* is not recommended and in any case the prior permission of the landowner must be obtained. There are a few camp sites, including one at Foxhole Barn in the Cuckmere valley and simple overnight accommodation in the manner of the French *gîte d'étape* is available at Foxhole and at the National Trust's Gumber Bothy, near Bignor Hill. The Society of Sussex Downsmen and the South East England Tourist Board both publish accommodation guides.

Public transport is better in some parts of the area than in others. Most of the principal towns are served by British Rail and it is possible to combine rail travel with walking in the eastern downland between Brighton and Eastbourne. The useful Arun Valley Line from London via Horsham to Bognor Regis provides access to the South Downs at Amberley and Arundel. If you are planning an expedition that involves using British Rail on a Sunday, always check first to see whether the service is disrupted by engineering works.

Country bus services are now less common than they were, but there is a reasonable service between Winchester and Petersfield and between Brighton and Eastbourne. In the summer, 'hop-on, hop-off' services operate from Brighton and Worthing. Bear in mind

To Winchester . . .

that taxis are now much more widely available than they used to be and it may be worth paying for one if the alternative is an unwelcome addition to the day's walk or the prospect of a journey by unreliable public transport.

The best beers available in the South Downs are brewed by Harvey's of Lewes and Gale's of Horndean.

COUNTRY CODE

Enjoy the countryside and respect its life and work
Guard against all risk of fire
Fasten all gates
Keep dogs under close control
Keep to public paths across farmland
Use gates and stiles to cross fences, hedges and walls
Leave livestock crops and machinery alone
Take your litter home
Help to keep all water clean
Protect wildlife, plants and trees
Take special care on country roads; keep to the right and walk in single file
Make no unnecessary noise

RIGHTS OF WAY

There are two main kinds of public rights of way: footpaths, open to walkers only, and bridleways, open to walkers, horse-riders and bicycle-riders. Footpaths are sometimes waymarked with a yellow dot and bridleways with a blue dot. Another category is byways, or 'roads used as a public path', and these can be used by walkers, horse-riders, cyclists and motor vehicles.

It is permissible to take a pram, pushchair or wheelchair along rights of way, and a dog if kept under control. You are also entitled to make a short detour around an obstruction, or remove it in order to get past.

There are also a number of other areas to which the public are allowed access by established custom or consent, and these include country parks and picnic sites, beaches, canal towpaths, some woodlands and forests, particularly those owned by the Forestry Commission, and many areas of open country. For more information about walking and the law contact the Countryside Commission (address on page 132). It is worth remembering that hedges and fences can be removed, rights of way re-routed, paths become very overgrown, and in wet weather conditions streams and rivers may be impassable.

. . . from Eastbourne

BEFORE YOU GO

Careful planning, adequate footwear and appropriate clothing are the keys to enjoyable walking. Although the South Downs Way poses no real problems in terms of terrain or weather conditions, walkers should wear tough, non-slip shoes as chalk tracks can be hard on the feet in dry weather and very slippery in wet weather, take a lightweight waterproof and carry enough food and drink for the day. Allow yourself plenty of time and, as optional extras, pack a pair of binoculars, a good field guide or two and a compass.

AEROFILMS LIMITED

Aerofilms was founded in 1919 and has specialised in the acquisition of aerial photography within the United Kingdom throughout its history. The company has a record of being innovative in the uses and applications of aerial photography.

Photographs looking at the environment in perspective are called oblique aerial photographs. These photographs are taken with Hasselblad cameras by professional photographers experienced in the difficult conditions encountered in aerial work.

Photographs looking straight down at the landscape are termed vertical aerial photographs. These photographs are obtained by using Leica survey cameras, the products from which are normally used in the making of maps.

Aerofilms has a unique library of oblique and vertical photographs in excess of one and a half million covering the United Kingdom. This library of photographs dates from 1919 to the present and is continually being updated.

Oblique and vertical photography can be taken to customers' specification by Aerofilms' professional photographers. Due to the specific nature of the requirements of the Aerofilms guides, new photography has been taken for these books.

To discover more of the wealth of past or present photographs held in the library at Aerofilms, including photographs in this guide, or to commission new aerial photography to your requirements, please contact:

Aerofilms Limited
Gate Studios
Station Road
Borehamwood
Herts
WD6 1EJ
Telephone: 081-207 0666
Fax: 081-207 5433

Introduction to the South Downs Way

THE South Downs are a range of rounded, smooth chalk hills extending across southern England from Eastbourne in Sussex to the Hampshire basin. In the course of their 100-mile (160km) journey, the hills march ever closer to the sea and eventually reach the English Channel as the great white cliffs of the Seven Sisters and Beachy Head, towering above the sea and the famous red-and-white lighthouse.

The landscape of the Downs divides into three distinct zones. In Sussex, the scenery is characterised by a pattern of dip slope and escarpment, the land rising gently from the south to a ridge and then falling sharply to the north. East of the River Arun, the downland is open and relatively treeless, with striking views north over the Weald and south to the sea. Between the Arun and War Down on the Sussex-Hampshire border, the landform is essentially the same as is in the east, but there is more tree cover and the landscape is more secretive. West of War Down there is no longer a single ridge and the South Downs Way follows a series of high points in a rolling, open landscape.

For most of the route from Eastbourne to Winchester the Way follows an ancient ridgeway track which dates back to prehistoric times: early man preferred a path which kept to the higher ground and avoided the mud and misery of the soggy Weald. The hills are not high and the terrain is not demanding, but the Way provides interesting variety in both scenery and physical demands. Unlike

some other long-distance paths, the
South Downs Way benefits from
the mild climate of southern
England and may be enjoyed
throughout the year. Even though
traditional downland turf is now
rare, walking and riding on the
well-drained chalk hills is easy,
larks still sing and villages with
comfortable pubs are never too far
away.

All in all, this walk is one of the
best in Britain and a splendid
introduction to the joys of
exploring the English
countryside, either on
foot or horseback.

Eastbourne to Alfriston

COASTAL FOOTPATH VIA THE SEVEN SISTERS 11 miles (17km)

The South Downs Way is the only national trail which is a bridleway and can be enjoyed by horse-riders and cyclists as well as walkers. From Eastbourne to Alfriston the bridleway runs inland through Jevington (see page 26), but walkers may choose to follow the coastal footpath over the Seven Sisters to Cuckmere Haven and then up the valley of the Cuckmere River to Alfriston.

EASTBOURNE is situated in a sheltered bay with the South Downs rising steeply to the west. The Old Town, or Bourne, as it was known, grew up around the head of the valley of the Bourne stream as an agricultural community, with the downland providing extensive pasture and arable fields. The chalk provided flint for building, as did the outcrop of hard greensand which occurs on the coast between Holywell and the pier.

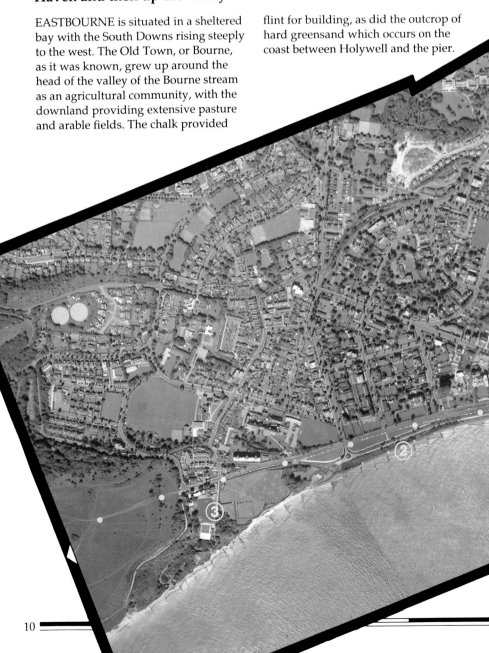

Eastbourne's Wish Tower is one of the Martello towers that was built along the coastline of Kent and Sussex during the Napoleonic wars

Although something of the medieval town remains, clustered round the late Norman parish church, it is the modern resort, prompted by the coming of the railway, that draws visitors to Eastbourne. In the mid-19th century over 90 per cent of the land in the parish was owned by two men, the 2nd Earl of Burlington (who became the 7th Duke of Devonshire in 1858) and Carew Davies-Gilbert. With the aid of the architect Decimus Burton and surveyors James Berry and Henry Currey, a comprehensive development plan was drawn up and successfully carried out.

As a result, Eastbourne has been described as an outstanding example of aristocratic seaside development and there is much to admire and enjoy in the town. Not least of its attractions are the 3-mile esplanade, the landscaped gardens, the sea-front hotels and the beach offering safe bathing. The Redoubt houses the Sussex Combined Services Museum, and there is a Butterfly Centre in the same street — Royal Parade.

EASTBOURNE

N

ROUTE DIRECTIONS

1. From Eastbourne pier walk, or take a bus, westwards along the front, past the Wish Tower.

2. Follow the road as it begins to climb up the hill past St Bede's preparatory school to arrive at the beginning (or end!) of the South Downs Way adjoining the Holywell Café in Foyle Way.

3. Alternatively, drive straight to the Holywell Café. Limited on-street parking is available nearby.

BEACHY HEAD marks the climax of the South Downs, the point where, after marching 100 miles (160km) from Winchester, the chalk hills eventually reach the sea — and in dramatic style. The great cliff, known to the Normans as *beau chef* (beautiful headland), rises over 500ft (150m) above the beach below, the red-and-white lighthouse providing both a foil and a scale.

The best place from which to appreciate Beachy Head is not the cliff-top but the beach. For the able-bodied, an alternative to the South Downs Way is to take the coastal footpath from the Holywell Café, reaching the beach at Cow Gap, from where, depending on the state of the tide, good views of the cliffs can be obtained. Return to Cow Gap and rejoin the path along the coast and, after a stiff climb, arrive at the Beachy Head Hotel.

Recent excavations at Bullock Down, north of Beachy Head, have revealed evidence of extensive early settlement in the area and the lynchets or earth banks marking the ancient field boundaries are clearly visible today.

Eastbourne Borough Council owns 4,000 acres of downland at Beachy Head. The land was bought to prevent it being developed and to preserve it as an amenity for local people. Currently it is largely managed as a commercial farming enterprise, although its unique value for conservation and amenity is now being recognised.

Beachy Head's distinctive lighthouse, built in 1902 to replace Belle Tout, further west, emits two flashes every 20 seconds. It is no longer manned

ROUTE DIRECTIONS

1. A sign just up the hill from the Holywell Café marks the beginning of the South Downs Way and provides some information about what is in store. The Way is marked by an acorn symbol and you will see several of these on your journey to Winchester!

2. Climb up the hill, bearing left where there is an opportunity and, following the waymarks, arrive above Whitebread Hole, where you can see some playing fields below.

3. Follow the waymarked path through the scrub, admiring views over the sea, and emerge near the Beachy Head Hotel where there are lavatories and a car park.

4. It is worth walking towards the cliff edge to get a view of Beachy Head lighthouse, but do be careful — the cliffs here are subject to constant erosion and the effects can be sudden and unexpected.

DUE NORTH of Birling Gap lies the village of East Dean, much expanded in recent years with suburban development taking place to the north of the A259, but retaining something of its old atmosphere around the village centre. Set back from the sea in a sheltered valley, East Dean provided a snug home for the local agricultural workers and folds for the downland sheep away from the wind and salt spray of the coast.

The village has an attractive green, flanked by The Tiger Inn and a number of brick-and-flint cottages. Of particular interest is The Dipperays, a Georgian brick house built for the notorious smuggler, James Dippery, who operated in this area. The 18th century saw the peak of smuggling activity in Sussex.

Before the introduction of income tax, government revenue depended on heavy indirect taxes on a wide range of goods. The temptations and rewards of illegally importing such materials were great and a highly organised industry developed as a result.

It was to lonely and isolated coves such as Birling Gap and Cuckmere Haven that small ships brought contraband at night, to be off-loaded on the beach and then conveyed secretly through Sussex to London, making use of a string of safe houses *en route*. Violence and bloodshed between the smugglers and the preventive men (represented in Lewes by Tom Paine, the radical politician) and between rival bands of smugglers was commonplace and the trade was only finally brought to an end by the French wars of the early 19th century.

> Them that asks no questions isn't told a lie — Watch the wall, my darling, while the Gentlemen go by.

ROUTE DIRECTIONS

1. Walk on to Belle Tout, the cliff-top building of Aberdeen granite which was the lighthouse for this part of the coast in the 19th century. It featured in a television adaptation of a Fay Weldon novel a few years ago.

2. Admiring the views westwards to the Seven Sisters, follow the waymarks along the cliff path and descend to Birling Gap, where there is access to the beach, parking, a café and a hotel.

Birling Gap has recently been bought by the National Trust and it has already taken steps to clear up an area which had become rather run down.

Since its days as a smugglers' hide-out the village of East Dean has sprawled inland and now has the population of a small town

BIRLING GAP

N

THE SEVEN SISTERS represent the very best in chalk coastal scenery and have been preserved for posterity as the result of the generosity and far sightedness of private landowners, the National Trust and East Sussex County Council. The National Trust owns 770 acres of chalk downland and cliffs at Crowlink and Birling Gap and the Crowlink Estate, which was once threatened by development, came into its hands as the result of gifts and private donations.

This coast was well-known to, and feared by, early sailors. Beachy Head itself was known as 'The Devil's Cape' by the Venetians because of its notorious reputation and the Seven Sisters appear under the name of the Seven Cliffes in a chart of 1588. The cliffs are Went Hill, Baily's Hill, Flat Hill, Flagstaff Brow, Brass Point, Rough Brow, Short Brow and Haven Brow: a total of eight, but Flat Brow is normally ignored to produce the alliterative seven.

Far below, the wave-cut platform extends out to sea and is visible at low tide. The sea-bed here and the life it supports is of considerable natural history interest and has been declared a voluntary marine nature reserve. A good impression of the dangers of this coast for sailors in small boats can be gained at Flagstaff Point where, at low tide, a treacherous bank of chalk rears out of the sea.

For the walker, the cliffs of the Seven Sisters are a paradise: cropped downland turf, wild flowers, larks singing, constantly changing and magnificent views, the excitement of proximity to the sea and the physical exertion demanded by the succession of 'brows' and 'bottoms' to be negotiated. It is an experience to be savoured and enjoyed, and not rushed. Many people choose to participate in the annual Seven Sisters Marathon; each to his own, but the world belongs to the man who takes his time.

Gulls, gannets, fulmars and terns wheeling overhead are the companions of the walker making his way over the famous Seven Sisters cliffs

ROUTE DIRECTIONS

1. From Birling Gap climb up the waymarked track and through a gate on to the National Trust's Crowlink property.

2. Follow the path over the Seven Sisters, the famous range of cliffs which stride along the coast between Birling Gap and Cuckmere Haven.

3. The ups and downs of the Seven Sisters present quite a challenge to even the most experienced walker: take plenty of time, relax and enjoy the views along the coast and out to sea.

CUCKMERE HAVEN

Undeveloped as it is, the Haven is an important site for estuarine wildlife

MOST OF this section of the walk crosses land owned by East Sussex County Council who manage it as a country park. The park extends to some 700 acres and includes both cliffs and the estuary of the Cuckmere River. At one time there was a caravan site at Cuckmere Haven and one of the objectives of the county council's management has been to clear away unsightly modern development so that visitors can enjoy the natural beauty of the area, the Haven being the only example in south-east England of an undeveloped estuary.

Information about the area is available in the visitor centre which has an exhibition and serves as the starting point for guided walks and other activities in the park. Camping facilities and simple overnight accommodation are available at Foxhole, to the east of the concrete road, and canoeing is possible on the meanders of the old course of the river. The estuary has a varied flora, with salt-loving plants such as sea-holly and sea-kale on the shingle beach and a variety of grasses and sedges inland. The area attracts many species of wildfowl, as well as migrant geese in the winter and herons in the summer.

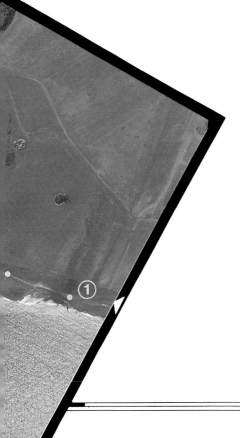

ROUTE DIRECTIONS

1. At Haven Brow, the last of the Sisters, pause to take in the view of the meanders of the Cuckmere River as it flows out to the sea at Cuckmere Haven.

2. The South Downs Way descends diagonally down the hill which is steep and can be slippery.

3. Make your way across the shingle bank to the mouth of the river and turn north, following the river bank towards Exceat bridge, where there is a pub. Turn right and, being careful to avoid the heavy traffic, walk to the information centre at Exceat (pronounced Excet).

4. To avoid the section on the main road turn off the Way before you reach the river bank and follow the concrete road to your right, which takes you straight to the information centre (although you still need to be careful crossing the road).

5. As well as the pub at Exceat bridge the information centre provides parking and lavatories, and you can pick up buses to Brighton and Eastbourne from here.

FRISTON FOREST is a Forestry Commission plantation extending to over 1,500 acres. Woodland is much less common on the South Downs in East Sussex than it is in West Sussex and Hampshire and some may feel that Friston Forest is out of place here amid the bare chalk downland of the Seven Sisters and Beachy Head. This impression derives partly from the fact that, although Friston is essentially a beech forest, when it was planted in 1926 considerable numbers of conifers were included to act as 'nurses' to the slower growing beech. As the conifers progressively reach maturity and are felled the beech forest will come into its own.

Leaving the Forest at Charleston Manor (the garden is open occasionally in the summer), views open out north up the Cuckmere valley to Alfriston and west to High and Over Hill (300ft, 90m) on the road from Seaford to Alfriston. It is possible to cross the river near the Plough and Harrow if you want to get to Frog Firle, Alfriston's youth hostel, which occupies a spacious country house dating from 1530. Frog Firle is a good base for walking and riding this part of the South Downs, with four other hostels within 20 miles distance.

If you continue through Litlington be careful as there is often no pavement. The village, famous for its tea gardens which have been enjoyed by generations of walkers, is largely built of brick and flint — the traditional building materials of the Sussex downland. The Norman parish church with its weatherboarded bell-turret lies at the north end of the village street.

| ROUTE DIRECTIONS |

1. From the visitor centre follow the South Downs Way signs up the hill and climb through a gap in a flint wall. There are good views from here back over the meanders of the Cuckmere River to the sea.

2. Climb down a long flight of steps to Westdean village. Take care as the steps can be slippery in wet weather or when it is frosty.

3. Walk straight on through the village and, following the waymarks, eventually turn left into Friston Forest.

4. The path emerges from the woodland on to open farmland near Charleston Manor. Press on north towards Litlington, joining the road near the Plough and Harrow pub.

5. The Way follows the road north to Litlington church, past the welcoming tea gardens and village store.

All Saints' Church can be seen to the right of the rectory, the oldest building in the pretty flint-built village of Westdean

ALFRISTON is a popular village and is perhaps best enjoyed outside busy holiday periods and summer Sunday afternoons. In its quieter moments it is a place of great interest, with a number of distinguished buildings. Historically, the village was the centre for the agricultural communities of the Cuckmere valley and the surrounding downland. Its importance is reflected in the size of the parish church of St Andrew, sometimes known as 'the cathedral of the Downs'. Built in the unusual form of a Greek cross, the church has a distinctive shingled spire which can be seen for miles.

Also in the village, and close by the church, is the Clergy House, a 14th-century Wealden hall house, half-timbered and thatched. The Clergy House was the first building to be acquired by the National Trust who bought it in 1896 for £10 and restored it with the help of the Society for the Protection of Ancient Buildings. The priests serving the parish would have lived together here, having one common hall or dining room and smaller apartments for individual use. When the house came into the Trust's ownership it had been altered almost beyond recognition through conversion into labourers' cottages.

Alfriston has a number of other good houses, many in brick and flint, and a Congregational chapel of 1801, reflecting the importance of non-conformity in the Cuckmere valley which, like Lewes and many Wealden communities, enjoyed a tradition of

ALFRISTON

independence in matters of religious belief. Two miles north of Alfriston is Drusillas, a small zoo with many attractions aimed at children.

Another building of interest in the area is Lullington church, just off the South Downs Way as you approach Alfriston from Litlington. Reckoned to be one of the smallest churches in England, Lullington is merely the chancel of a larger building, most of which has now disappeared.

ROUTE DIRECTIONS

1. Continue north from Litlington church towards Alfriston. After a while the Way leaves the road, rejoining it at a house called Plonk Barn.

2. At this point the coastal footpath via the Seven Sisters and the inland bridleway via Jevington join up and from now on the South Downs Way has bridleway status.

3. At Plonk Barn, turn left to cross the Cuckmere River by a white-painted wooden bridge, walk across The Tye — the open space beside the church — and you have arrived in Alfriston.

4. Leave Alfriston by the road called King's Ride Turn to page 32 to continue the walk.

CONTINUED FROM PAGE 30
5. Descend towards Alfriston and the Cuckmere valley. Follow the waymarks, cross one road and, at another, turn left. Follow the road to a house called Plonk Barn, turn right, cross the Cuckmere River by a white-painted bridge and arrive in the village of Alfriston.

Alfriston's church and the thatched Clergy House, by the watermeadows of the Cuckmere

THE COAST

Development of varying quality has sprawled along the coastal plain of Sussex practically without interruption and this view over Shoreham is typical. These days, for better or worse, marinas, holiday bungalows, factories and modern housing rub shoulders with long-established ports, old fishing villages and period seaside architecture

THE MARGIN where the land meets the sea has always been a zone of change and the coast of Sussex is no exception. The processes of erosion and accretion carry on more or less contemptuous of man's efforts to influence natural systems which he does not understand. In Sussex, coastal erosion continues to reduce the size of the Selsey peninsula and to push back the cliffs at Seven Sisters and Beachy Head, eroded material being carried eastwards and contributing to the build-up of Dungeness and the further isolation from the sea of the former ports of Winchelsea and Rye.

It was to the higher points on the coast and beside the broad tidal estuaries of the Sussex rivers that the early Saxon settlers were attracted. The suffix 'ing' is a Saxon place-name element and the string of places along the coast with this ending all date from this period. From these settlements, productive agricultural estates developed on the fertile coastal plain and on the Downs, areas which had been extensively cultivated by the Romans and in prehistoric times. The sea was of critical importance for trade and transport in the days before efficient land communications and was itself the source of fish for local consumption and export.

Until the 18th century, man's occupation of the downland coast of Sussex was limited to the small farming villages developed by the Saxons, the Channel ports, including Chichester, Arundel, Shoreham and Lewes, and the fishing town of Brighthelmstone. It was the proximity of Brighton (as it became known) to London and its relative ease of access by stage coach which led to its development as the prototype English seaside resort. Blessed with royal patronage by the Prince Regent, later King George IV, Brighton's popularity as a health resort with fashionable society led to its rapid expansion. With the coming of the railway and the arrival of working class day-trippers from London, Brighton lost its social cachet but consolidated its reputation as a slightly risqué holiday resort and as the major urban centre of Sussex.

The owners of land elsewhere on the Sussex coast sought to follow Brighton's example, but only at Eastbourne did this result in town development of quality. As the result of more recent development, the coast is largely built up from Selsey Bill to Eastbourne and this is where the bulk of the population of the county is to be found.

Beautifully kept gardens and handsome Victorian hotels and villas line the esplanade at Eastbourne, one of the resorts along the south coast that has retained its elegant appearance despite 20th-century pressures. The town has several buildings of note, and these include the pier built by Eugenius Birch

Part of Brighton's appeal is its multi-faceted character, but one of its most enduring and familiar charms is the breezy shingle beach with all its associated seaside entertainment. Fading Regency splendour, a dedication to tourism, thriving nightspots, cosmopolitan restaurants and lots of good shops are just a few of its other attractions

Eastbourne to Alfriston

INLAND BRIDLEWAY VIA JEVINGTON
7½ miles (12km)

ROUTE DIRECTIONS

1. To reach the beginning of the inland route make your way from central Eastbourne to Paradise Drive, the official start.

2. If you are proposing to ride the Way it is best to drive to the car park at Warren Hill as there is nowhere to leave a horse-box at Paradise Drive.

3. Climb up on to the top of the Downs, following the waymarks. Riders joining the Way from Warren Hill meet the official route at a trig point before the Way crosses the A259.

4. Having negotiated the main road, press on in a generally northerly direction and arrive eventually at a concrete dew pond.

The coastal route over the Seven Sisters involves some fairly strenuous walking and the average walker will find this stretch quite enough for one day. By contrast, the inland route via Jevington is considerably shorter and easier. Riders must use the inland route, walkers may choose either. Both have their own attractions and the wise walker will probably do both in the course of several expeditions on the South Downs Way, the choice being determined by the mood of the day, the weather and the preferred choice of lunch spot.

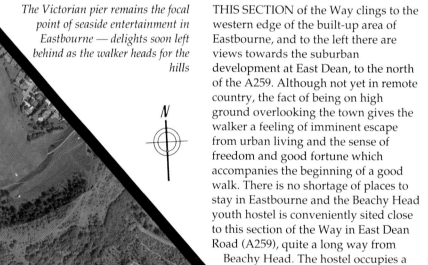

The Victorian pier remains the focal point of seaside entertainment in Eastbourne — delights soon left behind as the walker heads for the hills

THIS SECTION of the Way clings to the western edge of the built-up area of Eastbourne, and to the left there are views towards the suburban development at East Dean, to the north of the A259. Although not yet in remote country, the fact of being on high ground overlooking the town gives the walker a feeling of imminent escape from urban living and the sense of freedom and good fortune which accompanies the beginning of a good walk. There is no shortage of places to stay in Eastbourne and the Beachy Head youth hostel is conveniently sited close to this section of the Way in East Dean Road (A259), quite a long way from Beachy Head. The hostel occupies a former golf clubhouse and has good views across Eastbourne and Pevensey Bay to the east. A Southdown bus from the town centre passes the hostel.

THIS AREA of the Downs is particularly rich in archaeology. The whole of the South Downs contains evidence of prehistoric man's settlement, agriculture, commerce and industry and the traces of his occupation are often more readily revealed by aerial photography than from inspection on the ground. On this section of the walk you can make out the patterns of an ancient field system to the north of the South Downs Way between Bourne Hill and Jevington. These systems were based on the use of a primitive light

such as pottery fragments was washed down the fields and found its way into the lynchets, which are of great interest to archaeologists as a result.

To the north-east of Jevington lies Combe Hill (637ft, 190m), where there is a Neolithic causewayed enclosure and a number of barrows, or tumuli. The function of these causewayed enclosures is unclear. They may have been areas of assembly and trade, perhaps on the boundary of tribal territories, or used for exposure burials, in the manner of modern Red Indians. Some of them were occupied for extended periods, others were not.

JEVINGTON

plough, drawn by a small team of oxen. Only light soils could be cultivated in this way and these systems were common on the Downs where the chalk hills provided the right conditions.

The outlines of the fields can be traced in the landscape today because the boundaries of the small, squarish enclosures are marked by lynchets — banks of soil which have crept downhill under the influence of repeated ploughing and rain-wash to accumulate at the lower edges of each field. It was the practice to manure the fields with household and farm refuse and material

ROUTE DIRECTIONS

1. Press on north towards Bourne Hill, where there is a trig point at about 670ft (200m). This means you have climbed well over 300ft (about 100m) since the start of the walk in Eastbourne.

2. The South Downs Way bears west along a wide track between fences to Jevington, where there is a pub, The Eight Bells.

*There has been settlement at Jevington since
Saxon times and, although much restored,
much of the church dates from this period*

N

Many theories have been put forward as to why the Long Man was made, but whatever his original purpose he now serves as a notable landmark

WINDOVER HILL

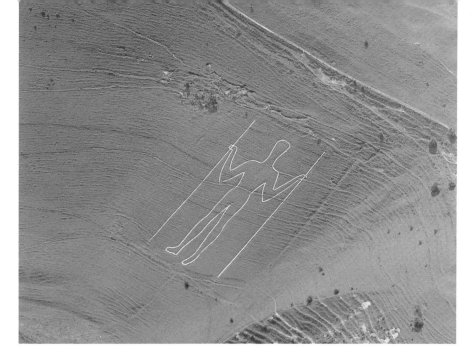

LULLINGTON HEATH, which is managed by English Nature as a National Nature Reserve, is an example of chalk heathland. This is an unusual habitat, heathland being usually associated with acid, sandy soils and not with chalk. The plants which grow here — including orchids and heathers — do not normally occur together and the ecology of the area is complex. The reserve extends to over 150 acres and is accessible only by public rights of way. Parties wishing to visit the reserve should contact English Nature at their office in Lewes.

The Long Man is a gigantic human figure cut in the turf on the steep face of the hill. Measuring 226ft (68m) in height,he (or she?) is reckoned to be one of the largest representations of the human form in the world. The figure is carefully designed so that, when seen from below, it appears well-proportioned, although close to it looks quite different. It may be seen to best advantage not from above on Windover Hill but from below in the village of Wilmington.Here there is a convenient public car park and, in the High Street, the remains of a Benedictine priory — now used to house an agricultural museum.

The earliest references to the Long Man occur in 18th-century manuscripts and no-one knows how old the figure is or for what purpose it was made.

ROUTE DIRECTIONS

1. From Jevington the Way climbs up again to a junction, where you take the second path on the left, which runs west and then north-west towards Holt Brow.

2. Before Holt Brow a bridleway leads off to the west through Lullington Heath National Nature Reserve to Litlington. Bear right and follow the Way in a generally north-westerly direction.

3. Continue to the top of Windover Hill (702ft, 210m), from which there is a grand view westward to Firle Beacon, Caburn and, in the distance, Chanctonbury Ring — sadly depleted since the 1987 storm.

4. You can take a footpath to the north, following the escarpment, and peer over the edge to get a view of the Long Man of Wilmington, the white figure carved on the hillside. This section of the walk joins the main path on page 22.

Alfriston to Lewes

13½ miles (22km)

The section of the South Downs Way from Alfriston to the Newmarket Inn, 2 miles (3km) west of Lewes, is one of the most spectacular on the whole route. It is also one of the longest, although it is quite feasible for the whole section to be tackled by an average walker in a day. There are plenty of places to stay in Lewes and buses to both Lewes and Brighton pass the Newmarket. Set off reasonably early in the morning from Alfriston and look forward to a full day in some of the best scenery the South Downs have to offer.

BOSTAL HILL

THE MAGNIFICENT block of downland between the Cuckmere and Ouse valleys is a classic example of chalk landscape. The dip slope of the South Downs rises gently from the south, intersected by innumerable dry valleys, known here as combes, or bottoms, to the escarpment at about 700ft (200m), from which the land falls sharply to the fertile greensand plain below, with settlements and farms grouped along the spring line. The fertility of the land below is well-illustrated by the size of the medieval tithe barn at Alciston to which tenants in the area were required to bring a proportion of their produce as tribute to their landlords, the monks of Battle Abbey.

The word bostal describes a track running up the scarp face of the Downs.

South-east of Bostal Hill, Bopeep Bostal descends the slope to join an old coach road under the Downs. As an alternative to the South Downs Way, thirsty walkers may follow this route to Firle village (see page 34) and its welcoming Ram Inn.

About a mile east of Firle is Charleston Farmhouse, where Duncan Grant and Vanessa and Clive Bell, members of the Bloomsbury Group of artists and writers, lived during the 1920s and 30s. The house and gardens have been restored by a private trust and are open to the public at certain times.

The main street of Alfriston — where there are inns, tea shops and gift shops in plenty. The church lies to the left of this picture

ROUTE DIRECTIONS

1. Leave the Star in Alfriston High Street by a road called King's Ride.

2. Following the waymarking, climb up on to the crest of the escarpment at Bostal Hill (640ft, 190m), overlooking the village of Alciston with its famous tithe barn.

N

SEE PAGE 22 ①

LOOKING DOWN from the escarpment to Firle it is quite easy to make out the boundaries of the old park around Firle Place, although most of it is now cultivated. To the east there is a prospect tower or folly to which there is no public access. The Firle Estate belongs to the Gage family and has done so for hundreds of years. It is open to the public on certain days during the summer.

Firle is a good example of what landscape historians call a closed village: dominated by the Firle Estate,

breed of sheep. Ellman farmed on his own account and was also steward of several estates belonging to his landlords at Glynde, the Trevors. He applied scientific methods to the improvement of the South Downs sheep and produced a breed renowned for the quality of both its wool and its meat. Southdown were exported all over the world but the size of the domestic flock was drastically reduced as the result of the South Downs being ploughed up for cereal production during and immediately after the Second World War. As a result, only 10,000 ewes were put to the ram in 1945, compared with a peak of 115,000 in 1911.

FIRLE BEACON

which provided accommodation and employment, the development of the village was highly controlled and it was difficult for outsiders to move in. The Gage family were traditionally Roman Catholics, in contrast to the Protestant Morleys who lived at Glynde Place on the other side of the valley. This house, too, can be visited.

Glynde, nestling below Mount Caburn, was the home of John Ellman (1753-1832) who was responsible for developing the famous Southdown

From Firle Beacon Glynde Reach, now a mere stream, can be picked out flowing in the valley at the foot of Caburn to join the Ouse. In earlier times the Ouse valley was probably a broad tidal inlet surrounding the great chalk outcrop of Caburn on three sides. Not surprisingly, Mount Caburn was chosen as a defensive site by early man.

Firle Beacon, a highspot of the Way both literally and in terms of views

ROUTE DIRECTIONS

1. The Way climbs gently up to Firle Beacon, at 713ft (217m) one of the finest view points on the South Downs, with the Weald to the north, the sea to the south, Caburn to the north-west and the valley of the River Ouse to the west.

N

TO THE NORTH, at Preston Court Farm, near Beddingham, aerial photography recently revealed the existence of a Roman villa, which has now been excavated. The building, 130ft (40m) long by 65ft (20m) wide, is a villa of the winged corridor type and was built during the late 2nd or early 3rd centuries. Historians believe that the place-name element 'comp' may indicate the boundary of a Roman agricultural estate and it is interesting that there is a Comp Farm just to the north-west of the villa. The villa is on private land and there is no public access.

The Romans left an indelible mark on the landscape of the South Downs. With major landing beaches, harbours and supply bases at Fishbourne and Pevensey, the Roman army swiftly established control of the Downs and the coastal plain of Sussex, both of which they found highly productive, especially for cereals. Southern England became a major granary of the Roman Empire and rich agricultural estates were farmed in Sussex, centring on grand houses and settlements such as the villas at Bignor, Angmering and Eastbourne, as well as here at Beddingham.

So efficient were Roman agricultural methods that it is calculated that the population of Britain under their influence rose to several millions, a figure not reached again until the late Middle Ages.

The Downs as well as the plain were intensively farmed during this period, with much further woodland clearance taking place. Today, we tend to think of sheep pasture as the traditional use of the downland, but there is little doubt that intensive arable production on the Downs is not a recent phenomenon: the Romans were at it 2,000 years ago and the traces of their activity abound — in villas, some field patterns, roads and even an occasional temple, as at Chanctonbury Ring.

ROUTE DIRECTIONS

1. Walk on along the crest of the escarpment past the car park at the top of Firle Bostal to the radio masts on Beddingham Hill.

2. The South Downs Way bears south-west and begins the descent of Itford Hill into the Ouse valley, with views to Lewes to the north and to Newhaven and the sea to the south, with the ribbon of the river linking the two.

BEDDINGHAM HILL

Beddingham Hill, and a view south across to the coast

The River Ouse meandering down to the sea at Newhaven

THIS SECTION of the route, which involves the crossing of the second major valley cutting through the South Downs, provides great contrasts in scenery, from the heights of Beddingham and Itford Hills to the river meadows of the Ouse valley at Southease. The river valley was once a branch of the sea, Lewes a major port,

Southease and Piddinghoe fishing villages and the two Rises of the Lewes Brooks small islands in a broad and shallow estuary.

The green at Southease is a good place for a rest. The church has an unusual round tower, as have Piddinghoe

church and St Michael's in Lewes. All are built of flint and one theory is that they may at one time have doubled as lighthouses, guiding vessels entering the estuary towards Lewes.

On the southern slope of Itford Hill lie the remains of an important Bronze Age farmstead consisting of 13 round huts, some of which archaeologists think were living huts and others workrooms and outbuildings. Beside the doorway of the largest hut, perhaps where the headman lived, was found a large carved chalk phallus, the traditional and universal symbol of fertility.

As the result of the use of the Downs for sheep pasture a great deal of archaeological evidence survived until destroyed by deep ploughing in the last 50 years. Much still remains, but continued ploughing has resulted in many ancient features which survived before the last war being lost or at least severely damaged. It is vitally important to conserve what remains but this will not happen unless the land concerned is brought into public ownership or farmers are paid realistic subsidies not to plough archaeological sites.

Southease church, one of only three round-towered churches in Sussex. There are interesting medieval wall paintings inside

SOUTHEASE

N

ROUTE DIRECTIONS

1. Follow the Way down Itford Hill and cross the busy A26 Lewes to Newhaven road at Itford Farm, where there is a water tap and a trough.

2. The farm track leads to the railway line, which the Way crosses at Southease Halt. Follow the track over the bridge crossing the River Ouse and arrive on the green by Southease church.

3. If you are walking and want to avoid the section of the South Downs Way which follows the road from Southease to Rodmell, turn right after the bridge and follow the riverside footpath for about a mile (1.5km) and then turn left to Rodmell when you meet a bridleway.

RODMELL is a secretive village and reveals little of itself from the busy main road. The traveller with time on his hands will find a delightful Norman parish church, a pretty Victorian village school with gables and bargeboards and many brick-and-flint cottages, some of them thatched. Monk's House, now owned by the National Trust, was the home of Leonard and Virginia Woolf from 1919 until his death in 1969. A number of members of the Bloomsbury Group of artists and writers lived in the area, including Duncan Grant and Vanessa Bell (see page 32). Finally overwhelmed by the depression that dogged her all her life, Virginia drowned herself in the Ouse at Southease in 1941.

Some 2½ miles (4km) south-west of Rodmell is the charming village of Telscombe. Now owned by Brighton Borough Council and protected from development, the village was in danger of being overwhelmed by the expansion of Peacehaven, the new settlement on the cliffs between Newhaven and Rottingdean which was allowed to occur in the days before effective planning control. Telscombe retains its old atmosphere and has a Tye, or green, like Alfriston. There is a youth hostel here and walkers and riders can best reach the village by following the bridleway through Cricketing Bottom.

ROUTE DIRECTIONS

1. There are one or two sections of the South Downs Way where the route follows busy roads and walkers and riders dice with death in the heavy traffic. The stretch from Southease to Rodmell is one of these and the greatest care is needed. An alternative route for walkers is available (see page 39), which is safer and more enjoyable, if a little longer.

2. Following either the road or the alternative footpath, make your way to the Marquess of Abergavenny pub at Rodmell. The village is well

worth exploring and it may be possible to visit Monk's House, home of the writer, Virginia Woolf.

3. Climb up Mill Lane, opposite the pub, to Mill Hill, where the Way turns at right angles and follows the crest of the escarpment north-west to Front Hill and Iford Hill.

The long, straggly village of Rodmell lies in the fertile valley of the Ouse

RODMELL

N

THIS SECTION of the route follows a high, open ridge with views east to Lewes and the Ouse valley and north-west to Ditchling Beacon. The settlements of Iford, Swanborough and Kingston lie in the lee of the Downs. The University of Sussex, one of the new universities founded in the 1960s, is at Falmer, between Lewes and Brighton, and Swanborough Manor, a medieval building altered and extended in the 15th century, is the official residence of the Vice-Chancellor.

The dew pond on Kingston Hill has been restored by young people from a local school, advised by the county council's countryside staff. Water supply has always been a problem on the South Downs. Rain falling on the chalk is absorbed into the ground and eventually finds its way to the water table, emerging as springs to the north of the escarpment. In the absence of streams or ponds naturally occurring on the hills, it has always been necessary for man to make arrangements to provide water for the livestock he wished to keep on the Downs. Dew ponds were an early response. They involved excavating a saucer-shaped depression and lining it with puddled or saturated clay to retain rainwater. The Downs were dotted with such ponds until the drive to eliminate tuberculosis resulted in piped supplies to water troughs.

ROUTE DIRECTIONS

1. Walk on along the crest towards Swanborough Hill (600ft, 180m), enjoying the open views to Lewes with its Norman castle commanding the crossing of the River Ouse.

2. Two or three paths lead down to Kingston and tired walkers and riders who are anxious to reach Lewes may take a short cut through the village.

3. At the junction with a bridleway, past the dew pond on Kingston Hill, the South Downs Way bears left, following the old route used by the fishwives of Brighton when taking their produce to sell at Lewes.

4. Walk on towards the radio mast on Newmarket Hill but turn right where the South Downs Way swings round to the north-west to descend to the A27 at the Newmarket Inn.

Kingston-near-Lewes

Lewes, showing the castle mound with its stone keep and the High Street with the round-towered Church of St Michael to the left of the picture

LEWES was one of the sites chosen by Alfred the Great for the location of the burhs or forts which he built to defend his kingdom against the Danes. Other examples include Winchester, Chichester and Burpham. Here at Lewes, the site was on top of the hill overlooking a convenient crossing point of the tidal River Ouse. The Normans immediately recognised the strategic importance of the site and William de Warenne, to whom the Rape of Lewes was entrusted by the Conqueror, raised his castle on a mound, or motte, within the burh.

A very unusual feature of Lewes Castle is that it has two mottes, one crowned by the stone keep, which is well worth climbing, and the other, known as Brack Mount, now unoccupied. In Barbican House, below the castle, the Museum of Sussex Archaeology portrays the town's history and displays antiquities from all over Sussex. Other aspects of domestic life in the county are recalled in the folk

museum in Anne of Cleves House, in Southover High Street.

Once established as the military and political capital of the area, Lewes developed as a market centre and as a port. Timber, hides and iron from the Weald and sheep and corn from the Downs were bought and sold at Lewes markets. Manufactured goods were brought in by coastal shipping, up the tidal estuary to the wharves and warehouses below the town's bridge. Travellers on foot and horseback, and carts and packhorses making their way across Sussex were channelled into the town in order to negotiate the river by the only available bridge. The 18th and early 19th centuries saw the development of Lewes as a fashionable county town, with social life centring on the assizes, the races and the two principal inns of the town, the Star and the White Hart.

Following the burning of a group of Protestant martyrs in the town under Mary I, Puritanism developed strong

roots in Lewes, a fact reflected today in the enthusiasm with which the town celebrates 5 November. The annual celebrations now have a social and community, rather than a religious, function.

ROUTE DIRECTIONS

1. Descend to the road at the Newmarket Inn where you can either catch a bus to Brighton or Lewes, or walk to the latter along the busy A27 past the entrance to Ashcombe Farm. If you have to cross the road, do so carefully: the traffic comes along here very quickly indeed.

LEWES

2. A waymark on the north side of the A27 opposite the Newmarket Inn indicates the path, which climbs up through Ashcombe Plantation towards Balmer Down.

Lewes Castle has wonderful all-round views, which include the watermeadows of the lower Ouse valley, and a climb to the top of the mound shows why William de Warenne chose the site, as well as providing a bird's eye view of the town. His successors gradually strengthened the original wooden castle with stone walls, towers and a keep. Some Norman architecture has survived, but much of what we see now is the result of 19th-century restoration following a long period of neglect

CASTLES AND FORTIFICATIONS

EARLY MAN established his strongholds on the high places and the South Downs are marked by a whole string of enclosures and hillforts with a history stretching back into the mists of antiquity. Of particular note and significance are the fortifications on Old Winchester Hill, near Exton, The Trundle above Chichester, Cissbury Hill near Worthing, Whitehawk on Brighton's Race Hill and The Caburn, near Lewes. All can be visited and some have been at least partially excavated, so something about their origins and purpose is known. Whether they were used for permanent settlement, for occupation in time of trouble or as places of assembly for cultural or religious purposes, they certainly must have been impressive structures in the landscape, their chalk and turf ramparts topped with wooden palisades and revetments.

When Alfred sought to defend his kingdom of Wessex against the Vikings he ordered the construction of a number of forts or 'burh's on the South Downs,

Of all the castles built to defend the Rapes of Sussex, that at Bramber has stood the test of time least successfully. However, its strategic position can still be appreciated from the ruins, commanding as they do good views of the River Adur

Pevensey, just east of Eastbourne, was where William landed in 1066 with his army. The Conqueror entrusted the Count of Mortain with the Rape of Pevensey, and the substantial castle ruins we see today are those of the count's fortress built within the remains of the Roman fort of *Anderida*

including those at Winchester, Chichester, Burpham, near Arundel, and Lewes. Sussex was divided into a series of vertical blocks of land for military and administrative purposes, related to the location of the burhs. These Rapes, as they were called, were adopted by the Normans as the basis of their government of Sussex, that county and Hampshire being of critical strategic importance lying as they did between the Duchy of Normandy and the rest of the Normans' new possessions in England.

The Rapes were entrusted by Duke William to his most reliable associates and relatives, men such as his cousin, Roger de Montgomery, and his possible son-in-law, William de Warenne. These lords constructed castles to defend their territories, usually on the same sites as those chosen by Alfred. In the case of the defence of the Arun valley, Montgomery chose to build, not at Burpham, but at Arundel on the west bank of the river. The early timber motte-and-bailey structures were replaced by substantial stone castles, often using material from the famous quarries at Caen in Normandy, shipped over the Channel through the Sussex ports.

The best preserved of the Norman castles of the Sussex downland is probably Lewes. Little remains above ground of Bramber, built to defend the Adur valley, but the site is well worth visiting. Only the motte remains of Chichester castle (in Priory Park) and Arundel is largely a 19th-century reconstruction, although some original work can be seen.

Roger de Montgomery, lieutenant to William the Conqueror, built a castle at Arundel to command the river crossing. Besieged by Parliamentary forces in the Civil War, it was severely damaged and very little of the original fortification has survived. After being restored at various times over the years the castle was virtually rebuilt in its present Gothic style at the end of the 19th century by the 15th Duke of Norfolk

Lewes to Devil's Dyke

11 miles (17km)

This section of the South Downs Way is a reasonably easy stretch for the average walker. The route creeps round the back of Brighton and Hove, and for most of the day you are conscious of being rather too close to Sussex's biggest urban centre and its new bypass. Having said that, the walk provides splendid views north over the Weald, a chance to visit a windmill and a village church with superb medieval wall paintings, a glimpse of the delightful Saddlescombe Farm with its donkey wheel, and the prospect of a cup of tea or a pint at journey's end.

ROUTE DIRECTIONS

1. The Way eventually turns north to reach the crest of the escarpment just to the west of Blackcap (677ft, 206m), recognisable by its crown of trees, replanted in 1953 to commemorate Queen Elizabeth II's coronation.

2. The route turns sharply west and follows the crest along Plumpton Plain towards Streat Hill.

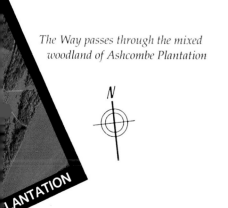

The Way passes through the mixed woodland of Ashcombe Plantation

N

EAST OF BLACKCAP is Mount Harry and the site of the Battle of Lewes, fought in 1264 between King Henry III and the barons led by Simon de Montfort. The King and his troops held the castle and the town, ignoring the high downland to the north-west. It was here that de Montfort deployed his forces. On the down above Lewes he knighted a number of his followers and, after attempts to make peace failed, battle was joined on the morning of 14 May. The King's forces were quickly defeated, with only a few knights and gentlemen being killed. Some 600 foot-soldiers, however, lost their lives. The battle led to a treaty between the King and the barons which is regarded as one of the first steps towards parliamentary government.

Mount Harry may be named after the King or, more likely, it may have the same origin as Harrow Hill, north of Worthing, indicating the location of a pre-Christian religious site (hearg: a heathen place of worship).

THE VIEWS north over the Weald from this stretch of the route are magnificent and may well have been what Rudyard Kipling had in mind when he wrote:

> No tender-hearted garden crowns,
> No bosomed woods adorn,
> Our blunt, bow-headed, whale-backed Downs,
> But gnarled and writhen thorn —
> Bare slopes where chasing shadows skim,
> And, through the gaps revealed,
> Belt upon belt, the wooded, dim,
> Blue goodness of the Weald.

This clump of beech trees was planted above Plumpton in 1887 to commemorate Queen Victoria's golden jubilee. It is not visible from the Way

From here you can see for miles towards the North Downs. Note how wooded the landscape is in the Weald compared with the relatively treeless Downs; not surprising, really, as the word Weald is related to the German word for forest, 'wald'. The Weald and the Downs form quite distinct regions with sharp differences in geology, drainage, vegetation, agricultural use and patterns of settlement. It is in the contrast between these two regions that much of the charm of the Sussex landscape lies.

Immediately below is the village of Plumpton, with its agricultural college and racecourse. A little further away, to the north-west, is Ditchling, a popular village with people who work in Brighton but want to live out of town. Ditchling has long been associated with the Arts and Crafts and residents earlier this century included Eric Gill and Frank Brangwyn.

Due east of Ditchling is the village of Streat, which lies on the old Roman road that ran east from Hassocks, itself an important Roman settlement. The name of the place derives from its location beside the old road, or street. Similar

PLUMPTON

Plumpton racecourse, used chiefly for national hunt racing

associations account for the names of Strettington, near Chichester, and Streatham, near Steyning. Other place-names in the countryside to the north, such as Plumpton Green and Wivelsfield Green, suggest the wooded nature of the Wealden landscape and the establishment of settlements in clearings in the ancient forest.

ROUTE DIRECTIONS

1. Walk west along the crest of the scarp slope towards Ditchling Beacon.

2. Paths to the right run down the slope to the village of Plumpton, where there is a pub and a shop.

THERE ARE a number of burial mounds, or tumuli, along this stretch of the route and, to the north-west of Ditchling Beacon, an ancient covered way or trench, known as the Slype, descends the escarpment. Its function is unclear.

Below, along the spring line, two streams set off from Whitelands and Park Barn Farm on their long journey to the sea at Shoreham. They join at Keymer to become a tributary of the River Adur. Keymer means 'cow pool' and the low-lying land here was presumably originally a watering place for cattle. Situated as it is on a rich band of gault clay, the area is traditionally important for the manufacture of bricks and tiles, and Keymer hand-made clay tiles and fittings are still manufactured at Burgess Hill. How important it is that these traditional industries survive if we are to retain anything of the local variety which is such an essential feature of English building styles.

The present county boundary at Keymer Post was established in 1974. Before that, the division was further west, at Edburton Hill, where an old motte-and-bailey castle marks the boundary between the Rapes of Lewes and Bramber. The Mid Sussex area was transferred to West Sussex as the result of the most recent reorganisation, although Brighton and Hove remain in East Sussex.

ROUTE DIRECTIONS

1. Cross the busy road to the car park at Ditchling Beacon. Not so long ago this was a flinty track leading over the Downs from Ditchling. Now it is used by heavy traffic and great care is needed.

2. The car park is owned by the National Trust, to whom the land was given in memory of a young airman killed in the Second World War.

3. Walk on along the crest, following the level path for about 2 miles (3½km) towards the windmills on Clayton Hill, enjoying the splendid views to the north.

4. *En route*, at Keymer Post, you cross the county boundary between East and West Sussex. The transition is apparent from the difference in the style of waymarking in the two counties.

5. As an alternative, it is possible to follow a waymarked path south from Ditchling Beacon to Lower Standean, rejoining the South Downs Way at Keymer Post.

Ditchling Beacon, the third highest point on the Downs, was the site of one of the fires lit at the time of the Armada

Two familiar Sussex landmarks — Jack, a tower mill and Jill, a post mill

A HUNDRED YEARS or so ago the Sussex landscape must have bristled with windmills, with a mill on almost every hill or eminence of any size. Early prints of Brighton show the town ringed with windmills. Many were on the Downs, but few remain today. To find two together, as at Clayton, is most unusual and certainly unique in Sussex. The wooden post mill, which is the smaller structure, was originally built in Brighton in 1821 and in 1850 was hauled by a team of oxen across the Downs to Clayton. The larger brick-built tower mill was put up in 1876. The two mills worked in tandem for a while and soon

came to be known as Jack and Jill.

Jack has since been incorporated into a private house, once the home of the golfer, Henry Longhurst, but Jill has been beautifully restored by a trust led by a vigorous local headmaster. Opening times are displayed at the mill.

For the energetic, a detour to Clayton village is well worthwhile. The church contains a series of medieval wall paintings unique in England for their extent and preservation. They are probably by the same artists who decorated the churches at Hardham, near Pulborough, and Coombes, in the Adur valley.

CLAYTON

N

ROUTE DIRECTIONS

1. Continue on towards the windmills on the top of Clayton Hill. Jack, a tower mill, is privately owned and not open to the public, but Jill, a post mill, can be visited at certain times.

2. There is a public car park beside the windmills and, at the point where the South Downs Way turns sharp left just before the mills, it is possible to pick up a bridleway which descends the escarpment to Clayton village, enabling the traveller to visit the parish church and the Jack and Jill pub. Pleasure must be paid for, however, and it is a steep climb back up to the top again.

3. Follow the Way due south and then west through Pyecombe golf course to cross the A272.

4. Walk through Pyecombe village, with its parish church and Plough Inn, and cross the busy A23 by the riding stables.

THE CLIMB over West Hill is quite strenuous but there are good views from the top east to Clayton Hill across the valley through which the London to Brighton road runs and west to the radio masts on Truleigh Hill. To the north can be seen Newtimber Hill, owned and managed by the National Trust.

Saddlescombe Farm, to which there is no public access, still retains something of the atmosphere captured in Miss Maude Robinson's account of her childhood there in the 1860s. Saddlescombe was a mixed farm with extensive fields of wheat, a dairy herd and three flocks, each of 300 sheep, kept on 900 acres: the rule then was 'a sheep to an acre'. The sheep were folded on arable land at night and during the day were supervised on the hills by the shepherds and their dogs. All labour was by hand, and the ploughing undertaken by teams of up to eight oxen. The animals worked in pairs and were always given names consisting of a single syllable and a double syllable: Hawk and Pheasant, Quick and Nimble, Crisp and Curly, and so on. Miss Robinson's book, *A South Down Farm in the Sixties*, is out of print but may be picked up in second-hand bookshops.

The Devil's Dyke is the steep-sided dry valley to the south of the hotel, which stands in an Iron Age hillfort. The area has been much visited since

Victorian times and earlier, mainly on account of the outstanding views from Dyke Hill across the Weald and along the escarpment of the Downs.

N

ROUTE DIRECTIONS

1. From Pyecombe the Way climbs up West Hill by a cart track past the riding stables, in a generally south-westerly direction.

2. From the summit of West Hill (733ft, 211m) drop down to Saddlescombe Farm and the busy road from Poynings to Brighton.

3. Cross the road carefully, bear left and then right by a raised reservoir and ascend Summer Down towards the Devil's Dyke Hotel, walking parallel with the road as far as the golf clubhouse.

4. Meet the road from Brighton, turn right and in about 100yds (100m) reach the hotel, with its car park, lavatories and buses to Brighton, where there is abundant accommodation, including a youth hostel at Patcham.

The tiny hamlet of Saddlescombe, pronounced locally as 'Salscum'

Devil's Dyke to Washington

11 miles (17km)

This section of the route negotiates the third river valley cutting through the South Downs, that of the River Adur — so called because of a fanciful association between the port of Shoreham and the Roman *Portus Adurni*. The traditional name for the river was the Bramber water, after the principal fortified settlement commanding the Adur valley as Lewes does that of the Ouse and Arundel that of the Arun. The route involves a level stretch on the crest of the escarpment to Edburton, Truleigh and Beeding Hills and a sharp descent to the floor of the valley at Botolphs. The Way then ascends Annington Hill, enters the Wiston Estate above Steyning and rolls on to Chanctonbury Ring and Washington.

EDBURTON HILL

Devil's Dyke, a hillfort during the Iron Age and now a tourist honey-pot

INTENSIVE arable production is the principal use of the agricultural land through which this stretch of the route passes. The area around Devil's Dyke is subject to intense pressure from visitors and is a favourite dumping site for unwanted household junk. A great line of pylons stalks across the landscape from the now defunct Shoreham power station and radio masts proliferate on Truleigh Hill. All these factors combine to produce a landscape which, as Lancelot Brown used to say, has the capability of improvement. But there is hope. The National Trust owns a significant chunk of the escarpment here and, by degrees, is reintroducing more sympathetic farming practices and dealing with some of the problems of erosion and litter. The Trust would like to buy more land to continue the good work and its South Downs Appeal deserves wide support.

Looking east along the escarpment from Edburton Hill

ROUTE DIRECTIONS

1. From the Devil's Dyke Hotel head west along the Fulking escarpment, which is owned by the National Trust.

2. The Way leaves the escarpment beneath an electricity power line and rejoins it at Edburton Hill. A short detour to investigate the remains of the motte-and-bailey castle to the north of the track is worthwhile.

3. From Edburton Hill (640ft, 192m) there are good views north over the Weald and west to Truleigh Hill with its collection of radio masts.

THE PRIMARY industry of the South Downs is agriculture but extractive industries are also important. Chalk has been quarried on the Downs for thousands of years. To the north of Beeding Hill there are extensive chalk workings and, to the south, Upper Beeding cement works and its associated quarry is a well-known blot on the landscape.

Chalk is an exceptionally pure form of limestone and was traditionally quarried for lime-burning and, to a lesser extent, for building stone. Lime was used as a dressing on the heavy clay soils of the Weald and to produce lime mortar. Chalk was also used for building, although its soft and perishable nature made it unsuitable for use externally. Hard chalk stone, such as that quarried at Pepper's works at Houghton Bridge, can be found in downland churches, including Burpham, near Arundel.

Chalk was quarried in all the river valleys cutting through the South Downs and the products were then transported by water, either inland to the Weald or downstream to the sea.

Throughout the downland, chalk pits of all shapes and sizes remain as evidence of an important industry of considerable value to the local economy and a source of local employment.

ROUTE DIRECTIONS

1. From Edburton Hill follow the Way to the radio masts on Truleigh Hill. Two of the masts have been there for some time, the third and largest arrived more recently. Designed to enable people to talk to each other on car phones, it is very visible from the road below the escarpment.

2. Continue on to Truleigh Hill youth hostel, a modern building set in 4½ acres of grounds on the site of the former Tottington Barn. The hostel is an ideal base for family and group holidays as well as an excellent overnight stop for walkers and riders on the South Downs Way.

3. The Way continues beside the long access road to Truleigh Hill to a small car park at the junction of a number of paths on Beeding Hill. Travellers wishing to visit Bramber and its castle should take the steep track to the north-west. The Way continues south-west into a field with the Upper Beeding cement works to the left.

Upper Beeding cement works and its quarry serve as a reminder that industry also plays an important role in the the economy of the South Downs

61

THE VALLEY of the River Adur has much in common with those of the Ouse and the Arun, with steep descents to the valley floor where the mature river meanders over a thickly carpeted alluvial plain. Two principal tributaries rise in the vicinity of Shipley and Burgess Hill respectively. They join at Bines Green, between Ashurst and Henfield, and then proceed to the sea at Shoreham, the present harbour entrance having been fixed in 1818. Historically, the Adur valley has a wide estuary, navigable by sea-going ships up to the ports of Steyning and Bramber where the Norman baron who was entrusted with this part of Sussex, William de Braose, built his castle.

Little of de Braose's castle, other than a tall fragment of the keep, remains above ground today. However, the site, which is now looked after by both English Heritage and the National Trust, is well worth visiting, as is the nearby parish church of St Nicholas, the patron

The rather sorry remains of Bramber Castle, onetime fortress of the Rape of Bramber built to guard the River Adur route inland from the sea

saint of sailors. The vicar of Bramber is also responsible for the little church of St Botolph. Appropriately, St Botolph is the patron saint of travellers.

ROUTE DIRECTIONS

1. The South Downs Way descends steeply from Beeding Hill to the busy A283 Steyning to Shoreham road.

2. Cross the road carefully and take the waymarked track which follows the road south to a water tap and horse trough provided by the Society of Sussex Downsmen for the refreshment of walkers, riders and their mounts.

3. The Way then turns sharply west to cross the River Adur by a modern bridleway bridge.

4. After a while you meet the start of the Downs Link, a bridleway which follows disused railway lines to Guildford, linking the North and South Downs Ways.

5. When you reach the road it is worthwhile diverting left to visit St Botolph's Church. Retrace your steps and follow the Way up the road past Annington Farm. Just past the farm, the Way leaves the road to the left and ascends Annington Hill.

6. Travellers who want to visit the village and castle of Bramber can do so by walking north up the Downs Link path from the village of Botolphs.

Annington Farm in Botolphs. St Botolph was an early missionary and the hamlet was named after the church (right of this view) dedicated to him

The Norman church and Church Street and High Street with their vernacular buildings can all be identified in this townscape of Steyning

THE ORIGINAL Saxon settlement of the Adur valley was at Steyning, said to have been established by St Cuthman when he got fed up with pushing his disabled mother in her cart from the West Country. The parish church was built on the spot where the cart came to a halt and, in the 12th century, was replaced by the splendid Norman building we can enjoy today, with its lofty nave and sturdy, decorated pillars.

The low-lying area to the north of the church, now in the process of being built on as development inexorably creeps out towards the bypass, was the site of the Saxon port. As the estuary progressively silted up the port moved to Bramber, then down river to Old Shoreham and, finally, to New Shoreham. The Manor of Steyning was given by Edward the Confessor to the Abbey of Fécamp in Normandy and the Norman monks continued to have considerable influence on the Steyning area throughout much of the medieval period.

The houses of Steyning are mainly timber-framed, making use of the plentiful oak of the Weald. Reeds from the river valley provided thatch and many thatched roofs remain in the village today. Sandstone from the greensand ridge just to the north was also a popular building material. The result is that Steyning is in harmony with its natural environment, a harmony which has survived pressures for change and development in recent years.

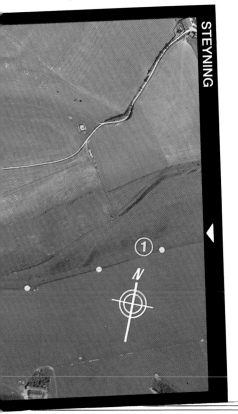

STEYNING

ROUTE DIRECTIONS

1. The path climbs up Annington Hill past Bramber Beeches, a clump of trees planted by the West Sussex Federation of Women's Institutes. West Sussex has strong associations with the WI movement: the first WI meeting in England took place in 1915 at Charlton and both the words and the music of 'Jerusalem' were written in the county.

2. At the top of Annington Hill the Way reaches the road from Steyning to Sompting. Taking care, turn right and follow the road north past Steyning Bowl, from where there are good views east over the Adur valley to Truleigh Hill.

3. The road eventually swings to the right and the South Downs Way continues straight on, past a flint memorial to a local farmer.

4. The Way continues over Steyning Round Hill (630ft, 189m), with the village of Steyning and its Norman church clustering below.

THIS SECTION of the route is largely on land owned by the Wiston Estate which has been in the hands of the Goring family for well over 200 years and is one of the larger privately owned estates on the Downs. There are significant estates in the eastern downland but, further west, land holdings generally tend to be on a larger scale, culminating in the Arundel, Norfolk, Goodwood, Petworth and Cowdray estates, some of them still of truly feudal proportions.

The viability of the Wiston Estate turns on the value of the mineral rights over its land to the north of Washington which is situated on a rich belt of Folkestone Beds sand, in great demand for building and other purposes. The sand workings are very apparent from the Downs, although one of the larger pits is being filled with refuse and restored to agriculture. The Goring family no longer live in Wiston House, which is let to the Foreign Office and used as a conference centre.

Chanctonbury Ring is an Iron Age hillfort which had a ring of beech trees planted on the ramparts in 1760. Unfortunately many of the trees were blown down in the1987 storm but this has provided the opportunity for further investigation of the archaeological importance of the site. From Chanctonbury, a black, sailless windmill can be seen at Rock, above the sandpits. This was the home of the composer, John Ireland, who was inspired by his love of this part of Sussex.

Many local legends and inexplicable happenings are associated with Chanctonbury Ring, which certainly has a strange mystical quality at times

ROUTE DIRECTIONS

1. Pass a trig point on the left and climb gently for about 1½ miles (2½ km) to Chanctonbury Ring, from which there are spectacular views north over the Weald and south to Cissbury Ring and the sea. This section of the route, particularly in the vicinity of Chanctonbury, can be wet, windy and cold.

2. From Chanctonbury Ring follow the Way which bears south-west away from the escarpment. Make a detour to visit the dew pond restored by the Society of Sussex Downsmen, which is on the right soon after the Ring.

3. At a T-junction, turn right and follow the Way down a steep chalky track, past an area where downland turf is being restored by sheep-grazing.

AT THIS POINT the Horsham to Worthing road runs through a gap in the Downs. The road lies at about 350ft (100m) above sea-level, compared with the height of the interrupted ridge of about 700ft (200m). This gap is similar to those carrying the Chichester to Midhurst road at Cocking Hill and the London to Brighton road at Pyecombe. Unlike the 'water gaps' carved by the rivers Cuckmere, Ouse, Adur and Arun, these are dry valleys and, of course, very much higher. They are known as 'wind gaps' and were formed by water run-off during the era when the Wealden dome of chalk, thrust upward in the great geological mountain-building period, was being eroded to produce the landform with which we are familiar today: the dip slopes and escarpments of the North and South Downs forming the lip of the Wealden district, exposing the sandstones and clays of the interior which we know as the High and Low Weald.

There is a bus service from Washington to Worthing, although it would be prudent to check the timetable in advance, and railway stations at Amberley and Pulborough, each about 6 or 7 miles (10km) away. The village also has a shop and a pub, of which Hilaire Belloc approved:

> They sell good beer at Haslemere
> And under Guildford Hill.
> But the swipes they take in at
> Washington Inn
> Is the very best beer I know.

ROUTE DIRECTIONS

1. Walk down the chalky track towards the A24 Horsham to Worthing road, passing a gas-pressure reducing station on the right, and arrive at a county council car park.

2. Here you have a choice: either to cross the busy dual carriageway road at this point and climb up Highden Hill or to take the old road (not the entrance to the quarry) north to the village of Washington.

3. The first option is probably shorter but the second enables the traveller to visit the Frankland Arms, the village and parish church of St Mary, to cross the A24 by means of a bridge and to make a rather more gentle approach back on to the ridge through Rowdell.

4. Whichever option is chosen the two routes merge at Barnsfarm Hill, about a mile (2km) west of the A24.

St Mary's Church at Washington. It was rebuilt in the mid-19th century

Formerly magnificent Cowdray House is little more than a shell since being devastated by a fire at the end of the 18th century, but the private estate remains one of the largest in Sussex. The house was built of local sandstone as a fortified manor. Today, the 600-acre park is a renowned venue for polo matches

The long gallery on the upper storey of Parham House was originally used as a children's play area and as a place in which to take exercise during inclement weather. Oliver Messel painted the ceiling. From the gallery there are good views over the deer park which has a lake and several statues

COUNTRY HOUSES

THE FERTILITY of the Sussex coastal plain and the availability of the Downs for pasture and of the Weald for timber and stock-rearing resulted in the early development of rich agricultural estates on the downland of Sussex and east Hampshire. In the west lay the great feudal estates of Cowdray, Petworth, Goodwood and Norfolk and, east of the Arun, the more modest, but nonetheless substantial, Parham, Wiston, Glynde and Firle estates. Each featured a substantial country house from which the business of the estate was conducted and which was designed both to provide domestic comfort for the proprietor and to impress tenants and neighbours with his substance and sense of style and fashion.

Cowdray was probably the grandest country house Sussex has ever seen. Built in a similar style to Hampton Court by Sir Thomas Browne, King Henry VIII's Master of Horse, the house was burnt down in 1793 and today the picturesque ruins are all that remains. A similarly disastrous fire destroyed the interior of Uppark, the National Trust-owned late 17th-century mansion on the Downs above Harting, in 1989. The National Trust also

Beautiful English and French furniture and a collection of impressive paintings fill the rooms of Firle Place. The house, built in the late 15th century by Sir John Gage, was completely remodelled 300 or so years later but has remained in the hands of the Gage family throughout its history. Built of soft-grey stone, it lies tucked away right at the foot of the Downs, partly hidden by woodland

owns Petworth House and its park. The present house was rebuilt in French style in the late 17th century and the grounds were designed by Lancelot (Capability) Brown. The 3rd Earl of Egremont was a great agricultural improver and supporter of projects designed to develop industry and commerce in the county in the late 18th and early 19th centuries. The Duke of Richmond runs his 12,000 acre downland estate from Goodwood House; the Norfolk and Arundel estates are managed from Arundel. Parham, an almost perfect Elizabethan house, was occupied by the Bishop family for 11 generations and the Wiston Estate has been in the hands of the Goring family for at least 200 years, although Wiston House is now occupied by the Foreign and Commonwealth Office, who run it as a conference centre. Glynde Place was built for the Morley family in the 16th-century and is now the home of Lord Hampden. The Morleys were for Parliament during the Civil War, whereas the Catholic Gages at nearby Firle Place were leading Royalists. The houses at Parham, Goodwood, Firle, Uppark and Petworth are all open to the public at certain times.

Petworth is a country house on a grand scale and one of the most famous in Sussex. The painting shown here adorns the ceiling above the main staircase, and throughout the rest of the house numerous works by Turner (a frequent visitor) and Van Dyck can be seen. The huge deer park provides good walks and the best view of the house

Washington to Arundel

13 miles (21km)

The Way proceeds west from Washington along the escarpment to Amberley Mount then descends to cross the Arun valley and climbs up to Bury Hill (430ft, 129m). From Bury Hill, paths lead through Houghton Forest and Arundel Park to the town of Arundel, some 3 miles (5km) away. Accommodation is available in Arundel and there are shops and a railway station. There is a youth hostel at Warningcamp, 1½ miles (2km) outside the town. This section of the route features good views north over the villages and the countryside of the Weald and south towards the sea. There is the chance to visit the Chalk Pits Museum at Houghton Bridge, near Amberley, which also has a railway station.

TO THE SOUTH-EAST can be seen Cissbury Ring, the great Iron Age fort on its isolated chalk hill to the east of Findon valley. The largest of the South Downs hillforts, Cissbury enclosed an area of some 65 acres within substantial ditches and ramparts. Also within the site are much earlier flint mines, the remains of an ancient industry of vital importance to early man.

Cissbury was one of the most important sites for mining and shaping flints in Britain, and implements from here were traded over a wide area. There is another important complex of flint mines on Harrow Hill, the right-hand of the twin peaks which are visible looking south from Chantry Post (the other is Blackpatch Hill). Some of the mines on Harrow Hill have been excavated and archaeologists found the deer antler picks used by the miners and even the soot marks left by their lamps on the roofs of the tunnels.

Views from Cissbury Ring, a National Trust property north of Worthing, extend east to Beachy Head and west across to the Isle of Wight

ROUTE DIRECTIONS

1. Follow the Way from Barnsfarm Hill along the crest to Chantry Post (630ft, 189m), where there is a car park and access by road from Storrington, the large village below.

2. Continue over Kithurst Hill (710ft, 213m) towards another car park. Along this section of the Way steps have been taken to prevent the pleasure of walkers and riders being spoiled by vehicle drivers, who are confined to the designated parking areas.

CHANTRY HILL

Below the wooded scarp of Springhead Hill lie the watermeadows of the Arun

TO THE NORTH, Springhead Farm is in the foreground. Located on the spring line, where water percolating through the chalk meets an impervious seam of gault clay, the little streams emerging from the scarp foot find their way through the watermeadows to join the Riven Arun.

Further north is Parham House set in its landscaped deer park. One of the best Elizabethan houses in Sussex, Parham is built in the traditional E pattern in honour of the Virgin Queen. The great hall is a particularly fine room but the feature many visitors most admire is the long gallery running the entire length of the house and with a beautifully decorated ceiling. From the Way, you can also pick out Parham church and the cricket pitch beside the lake. The topography of Parham Park resembles that of the field of the Battle of Waterloo, reconstructions of which take place here from time to time.

To the south the dip slope falls gently away to Wepham Down and Lee Farm, with subsidiary high points occurring at Perry Hill and Barpham Hill. In the North Downs the dip slope climbs up gradually and evenly towards the scarp and the chalk is covered with a layer of clay with flints, whereas in the case of the South Downs the landform of the dip slope is much more varied and pitted, the protective covering having been eroded away.

The parish of Burpham extends from the Arun valley north to the lower slopes of Rackham Hill. A series of good paths can be followed from Rackham Hill to Burpham village, to the youth hostel at Warningcamp, and to Arundel. These paths provide a convenient and shorter route to Arundel for those who wish to leave the South Downs Way at Rackham Hill. Burpham's name derives from the location of the Saxon burh or fort on the promontory of chalk extending into the river valley from the village pub.

ROUTE DIRECTIONS

1. Follow the South Downs Way past a car park, road access to which is from the Amberley to Storrington road near Springhead Farm.

2. The Way rises gently over Springhead Hill to Rackham Hill (643ft, 193m), surmounted by its clump of trees, formerly a favourite haunt of itinerant charcoal burners.

HERE THE ROUTE descends into the fourth river valley which cuts through the Downs, that of the Arun. In many ways, the Arun marks a boundary between the rolling, open landscape of the eastern section of the Sussex downland and the more wooded and secretive western Downs. The Arun is the major river of West Sussex and, with its tributary, the Rother, which joins the main river at Pulborough, drains a very large area of the western Weald. As a result, the river is very fast flowing. It is also tidal, the effects being felt up to Pulborough. In consequence, the Arun valley has traditionally been subject to extensive flooding in winter.

The area between Amberley and Pulborough known as the Amberley Wildbrooks was formerly managed as watermeadows and a proposal to drain the area in the 1970s was defeated after a successful campaign by conservationists. The area is now a Site of Special Scientific Interest and much of it is managed by the Sussex Wildlife Trust as a local nature reserve.

The village of Amberley is one of the showpieces of Sussex. From the South Downs Way, you can see Amberley Castle, at one time a summer residence of the Bishops of Chichester and now a restaurant and hotel. King Charles II

Although built to defend the upper reaches of the Arun valley, Amberley Castle never saw action. Now it makes a fine hotel and restaurant

stayed here in 1651 *en route* to France after the Battle of Worcester. Amberley station is at Houghton Bridge and there are trains north to Pulborough and London and south to Arundel and the coast.

ROUTE DIRECTIONS

1. From Rackham Hill descend gently to Amberley Mount and then much more steeply past Downs Farm to a road by a large Victorian house, formerly the home of the owners of the extensive chalk quarries to the south-west.

2. Follow the road, called High Titten, downhill to the busy Arundel to Storrington road. This is the most dangerous section of the whole of the South Downs Way

3. Taking great care, walk south on the main road towards Houghton Bridge. There is no pavement and cars and lorries come round the bend very quickly indeed.

Amberley, and the Arun which makes its way down through Arundel to the sea

THE COMPLEX of chalk workings at Houghton Bridge is the largest on the South Downs and, indeed, at its peak, was one of the largest producers of lime in Europe, employing over 100 men. Chalk has been dug and lime burnt here since very early times but became organised on an industrial basis under the control of the Pepper family in the 19th century. Excavation was by hand, the men working with unusual three-wheeled horse-drawn carts to transport the chalk to the lime kilns, where production was supervised by skilled lime-burners. The lime was transported by river and, with the opening of the Wey and Arun Canal in 1816, by inland waterways. This traffic transferred to the railway in due course and sidings ran from the main line into the quarries, although the wharf continued in use for many years. The quarries now house the Chalk Pits Museum which illustrates the industrial history of the area and is well worth visiting.

ROUTE DIRECTIONS

1. Follow the main road past the service entrance to the Chalk Pits Museum to Amberley station and the museum car park and main entrance. Weary walkers could take a train from here to Arundel, or walk into Amberley village, where there are a couple of pubs and limited accommodation.

2. The road continues under the railway bridge, past The Bridge Inn and the riverside tea gardens, where boats may be hired, and along a causeway to the village of Houghton.

3. Turn right and follow the road to Bury for a while and then turn left into a field and climb up through Coombe Wood to the A29 London to Bognor Regis road at Bury Hill (430ft, 120m).

4. Walkers wanting to divert to Arundel should cross the road carefully and follow the Way signs almost immediately opposite. After about ¼ mile (½km), a bridleway heads off south. Follow this path to the county council car park at Whiteways Lodge (where there are lavatories and refreshments), cross the roundabout carefully and, following the public footpath signs, walk round the lodge and enter Arundel Park. Follow the track (which shortly becomes a surfaced road) downhill all the way to Arundel.

The Chalk Pits Museum at Amberley, where industrial relics, a narrow gauge railway, a visitor centre and a nature trail can be enjoyed

Arundel to Cocking 14 miles (22km)

Starting from Arundel and rejoining the South Downs Way at Bury Hill, the route to Cocking is a good day's walk. From Bury Hill the Way climbs up towards the radio masts on Bignor Hill (816ft, 245m) and, after crossing the mainroad at Littleton Farm, climbs up again to Littleton Down, at 836ft (250m) the highest point on the South Downs in Sussex. The Way then rolls on over Graffham Down and Heyshott Down, dropping to Cocking Hill. After leaving the refreshment kiosk at Whiteways Lodge, the route is entirely on the high downland and, although it is possible to visit pubs and shops in the villages below the scarp, the inevitable consequence is a stiff climb back up to the ridge. It is therefore best to carry sufficient food and drink for the journey.

ARUNDEL, with its French Gothic cathedral and castle, commands the river valley of the Arun, as Lewes does that of the Ouse. The Rape of Arundel was given by William the Conqueror to his cousin, Roger de Montgomery, who chose this site to the west of the river for his castle in preference to the Saxon stronghold at Burpham. The town has a Toy and Military Museum, several antique shops, bookshops, lots of pubs and places to stay and is a good base from which to explore the Downs in West Sussex. On the outskirts of the town the Wildfowl and Wetlands Trust owns 55 acres of watermeadows where there are good facilities for visitors.

The villa at Bignor, which is open to the public, was discovered as early as 1811 and the structures erected to protect the mosaic floors are now themselves listed as buildings of historic interest.

ROUTE DIRECTIONS

1. Walkers should retrace their steps from Arundel through the Park to Whiteways Lodge and rejoin the Way at Bury Hill.

2. Head for a collection of black barns near Westburton Hill and follow the waymarks to arrive at the Toby Stone, a memorial to a local huntsman.

3. A bridleway leads north-west down the escarpment from the black barns to the village of Bignor, with its famous Roman villa. The nearest pub is The White Horse at Sutton.

4. Walk on towards the National Trust car park on Bignor Hill, which is accessible by road from Bignor and Bury.

Roman mosaic pavements and artefacts are preserved at Bignor's villa

ROUTE DIRECTIONS

1. From the car park on Bignor Hill follow the Way signs and cross Stane Street, the old Roman road from Chichester to London.

2. The Way runs south of the radio masts and the main escarpment of the Downs across Burton Down to the Chichester to Petworth road at Littleton Farm.

3. As an alternative, walkers may follow a series of bridleways along the main escarpment north of the radio masts, meet the road at Duncton Hill and make their way on footpaths to rejoin the Way north of Littleton Down.

The Neolithic camp lying just south of the Way at Bignor Hill

ON BIGNOR HILL there is a wooden signpost pointing the way north-east to *Londinium* and south-west to *Noviomagus*, the Roman name for Chichester. Built in four straight alignments, Stane Street ran for 57 miles from the East Gate of Chichester to London bridge. The first alignment is from Chichester to Pulborough bridge and may easily be followed on the ground. Particularly impressive is the 3-mile (5km) stretch from Eartham to Bignor Hill, along which there is a public right of way. There is a Forestry Commission car park at Eartham and from here it is possible to devise a triangular walk up Stane Street to Bignor Hill, south towards Slindon and then west back to the car park.

The importance of Roman Chichester as a port and commercial and administrative centre is reflected in the decision to provide the town with direct access to the capital. The road is constructed on a raised causeway, or *agger*, made of flints, rammed chalk and beach pebbles. There is a ditch on either side, the width of the whole road from centre to centre of the ditches being 86ft (26m). This arrangement may have been designed to avoid cover on either side of the road in which bandits might have concealed themselves.

Every 12 miles (19km) or so, representing a day's journey on foot or by ox-wagon, an inn or *mansio* was provided for use by travellers.

The National Trust, who owns the 3,500-acre Slindon Estate, has provided a present-day version of the Roman *mansio* at Gumber Farm, south-west of Bignor Hill. Accessible only by walkers and riders, the Gumber Bothy, as it is called, provides simple overnight accommodation and space for camping. Details are available from the National Trust.

THE DIP SLOPE to the south-west of the Way is known as Tegleaze. 'Teg' is a Sussex dialect word dating back to the 16th century for a young sheep and the second element of the name is derived

ROUTE DIRECTIONS

1. From Littleton Farm the Way climbs up a chalky track quite steeply to Littleton Down, the highest point on the South Downs in Sussex. Although only 64ft (20m) lower than Butser Hill, Littleton Down is quite a disappointment as the area is thickly wooded and there are few long views.

2. The Way is joined at this point by the footpath from Duncton Hill which brings walkers who diverted to follow the escarpment above Sutton and Barlavington back on to the main route.

3. Continue in a generally north-westerly direction over Crown Tegleaze with Seaford College and the valley of the River Rother to the north.

from a Saxon word meaning pasture. Together they produce 'tegleaze', which means land on the Downs over which there are rights to graze sheep. All this serves as a reminder, if any were needed, of the significance of the South Downs for sheep grazing, particularly in the recent past.

The intensity of stocking of sheep on the South Downs in the early 19th century surprised the Reverend Arthur Young, who reported to the Board of Agriculture on the agriculture of the county of Sussex in 1813. He calculated that, on the 200 square miles of downland between Eastbourne and Steyning, 200,000 ewes were kept — an average of 1½ sheep to an acre. Young attributed this high stocking-ratio to the general custom of wintering tegs, 'or lambs of last yearing', in the Weald in groups of 30, 40 or 50, the small farmers receiving the sheep being paid so much per head. Young studied the management of sheep on the Downs in considerable depth and, in discussing the folding of sheep on arable land, vividly describes the Sussex sheep flock as 'a moving dung-hill, manuring the land without any expense'.

Below the scarp, Seaford College now occupies Lavington Park, once the home of Bishop Samuel Wilberforce ('Soapy Sam') son of the anti-slavery campaigner. The clump of trees on Woolavington Down is known as Bishop's Ring for this reason.

Woodland on Crown Tegleaze means views are limited, but deer may be seen

②

THE RIVER ROTHER runs in the vale below the escarpment between the Downs and the sandstone ridge to the north. The youthful river rises near Liss in Hampshire and is fed by many small

ROUTE DIRECTIONS

1. The Way presses on westwards, mainly through woodland so the going can be wet and sticky. Part of the area is now managed for conservation by a group of volunteers.

2. Continue along the woodland path, past an intersection with a forestry track known as the Broad Walk, and, at the junction with a bridleway climbing up the escarpment from Heyshott, the South Downs Way turns left and then almost immediately right. Alternatively, you may wish to descend to Heyshott and its Unicorn Inn, before finding your way along footpaths to the village of Cocking, where there is a pub and a shop.

tributaries, one of which starts life as a spring below Graffham village. Supplemented by similar streams along its route, the river has become quite sizeable by the time it reaches Midhurst, where its rate of descent decreases. Eventually the mature river joins the Arun near Pulborough, but before it does so large quantities of water are abstracted, treated and pumped into the public water supply at the Hardham waterworks.

To the south, the wooded dip slope descends quite steeply into the valley of the River Lavant and then rises sharply again to the ridge on which The Trundle and Goodwood Racecourse are situated. The Lavant is now a winterbourne, flowing only when persistent rain has recharged the underground aquifer, of which it is in effect an overflow. Increased abstraction of water by boreholes and continuing shortage of rainfall have reduced the flow of this and other chalk streams and the Lavant now makes only rare appearances. The valley which the river carved in younger and happier days runs from Littleton Farm and Upwaltham through East Dean and Charlton to Singleton, where it changes course and runs due south to Chichester and the sea.

A path leads down through the trees on Graffham Down to Graffham church, which nestles right at the foot of the hill some way from its village

TO THE SOUTH lies the Duke of Richmond's Goodwood Estate. Once owned by the family of Harold Godwinson, the last Saxon king (Goodwood: Godwin's wood), the estate marches with the Cowdray Estate to the north and the West Dean Estate to the west.

Goodwood is famous for its racecourse and particularly for the 'Glorious Goodwood' July meeting, but racing is just one of the many successful enterprises managed from Goodwood House — a fine mansion containing numerous art treasures. The estate has always been conscious of the need to cater for the public's enjoyment of the countryside and of the importance of nature conservation. One of the earliest country parks was established here in the 1970s and Levin Down above

ROUTE DIRECTIONS

1. Follow the waymarked route to Heyshott Down where there is a group of Bronze Age barrows. A section of the escarpment here is managed by the Society of Sussex Downsmen. The work of their warden in clearing scrub and encouraging the return of downland turf is supplemented by the efforts of a dedicated band of members who are often to be found here.

2. The Way eventually leaves the shelter of the woodland and descends through open, arable land to Hill Barn, where there is a saw-mill and a number of buildings with yellow doors and window frames, indicating that you are now on the Cowdray Estate — probably the largest private estate on the South Downs — managed from Lord Cowdray's estate office at Easebourne, near Midhurst.

Cocking, bisected by the busy A286, forms part of the Cowdray Estate

Singleton is managed with conservation in mind.

Oil companies have been prospecting on the Sussex Downs for some time and a small oil well has now been established in Singleton Forest. More traditional extractive industry takes place in the chalk quarries on the north face of Cocking Hill, where the locally well-known Midhurst Whites bricks are made.

Some 2½ miles (4km) south of Cocking Hill is the Weald and Downland Open Air Museum at Singleton. Here vernacular buildings which could not be preserved on their original sites have been reconstructed and events such as steam ploughing and sheepdog trials regularly take place.

HEYSHOTT DOWN

CHURCHES AND CATHEDRALS

EVERY downland community had its parish church and the Church of England enjoyed undisputed supremacy throughout most of the South Downs, supported by an overwhelmingly Anglican and Tory squirearchy. Small but very important Roman Catholic centres – notable at Arundel and Slindon, and at West Firle – survived as the result of powerful aristocratic patronage. Dissenters were to be found on the Downs – for example, the Quakers at Saddlescombe who visited the meeting house in Brighton on Sundays – but, in general terms, Dissent flourished in the more egalitarian communities of the Weald and among tradespeople in the country towns; in the downland of Sussex and east Hampshire, the authority of the parson and the squire went largely unquestioned.

The downland churches which provided for the spiritual needs of the rural community were mainly of Saxon or Norman origin. One of the most interesting from an architectural point of view is the parish church at Sompting, with its unusual tower of a design more commonly found in the Rhineland. Particularly important Norman churches on or near the Downs include Boxgrove Priory, Burpham, Amberley, Steyning, Old and New Shoreham and the round-towered churches of the Ouse valley – St Michael's at Lewes and the parish churches of Southease and Piddinghoe.

The title 'cathedral of the Downs' is disputed between the parish churches of East Meon and Alfriston. Both are marvellous buildings in incomparable settings and it would be extremely difficult to make a choice between them. The title of the smallest church must go to Lullington, in the Cuckmere valley, which is but the chancel of a much larger church, now destroyed. The churches at Clayton, near Burgess Hill and Coombes, in the Adur valley, retain important medieval wall paintings executed, it is thought, by a band of itinerant artists based at Lewes Priory.

The Priory of St Pancras at Lewes was founded by the Norman lord, William de Warenne, and his wife,

John Piper's lovely *Tree of Life* window in Firle's tiny parish church commemorates the 6th Viscount Gage. There are alabaster effigies in the church of Sir John Gage, who built Firle Place next door, and his wife. Piper also designed the equally colourful altar-screen tapestry in Chichester Cathedral

Gundrada, from the great Benedictine abbey of Cluny in Burgundy, and was followed by the creation of dependent houses elsewhere in England. The Priory is now ruined, but excavations have revealed that the priory church was larger than Chichester Cathedral, the spire of which is an important landmark for travellers on the Downs in western Sussex. In the far west, the massive bulk of Winchester Cathedral dominates the approach to the city from Cheesefoot Head.

All Saints' at East Meon is one of the prettiest churches encountered along the Way, and its setting ranks equally high. Built of stone and flint, the church has an unusual spire of white lead, and its tower boasts three Norman arches on each side.

The close-up shows the west door. It is thought that the original church may have been built by Bishop Wakelyn, who was responsible for the first cathedral at Winchester

③ ②

ROUTE DIRECTIONS

1. From the small car park provided by the county council on the main road climb up Cocking Down, initially through some farm buildings. The chalky track is stony and can be slippery in wet weather.

2. On Cocking Down a bridleway crosses the Way, climbing up the escarpment from Cocking to the north-east and then heading south-west into West Dean Woods.

3. Skirting the woodland of Stead Combe to the south, the Way passes a trig point at 763ft (229m) and arrives at Linch Down. Below the scarp, the pretty underdown lane runs from Cocking through Bepton and Didling.

A panorama showing the use of the countryside around Cocking Down

Cocking to Butser

12 miles (19km)

This is a fine day's walk in some of the best scenery of the West Sussex downland, with views north over the Rother valley to Black Down and south to Chichester and the sea. There are particularly good, open views north from Harting Down, which is about half way, and the walk concludes at Queen Elizabeth country park on the A3 south of Petersfield and in the shadow of Butser Hill, at 900ft (270m) the highest point on the South Downs. Once again, there are few opportunities for refreshment *en route*, although there is a welcome café at Queen Elizabeth country park at the end of the day.

TO THE SOUTH of the scarp lies the West Dean Estate, formerly owned by Edward James, the eccentric millionaire and art connoisseur who established and endowed the Edward James Foundation. The Foundation runs West Dean House as a college providing a range of courses in arts and crafts, and the gardens are open to the public.

The estate is also run by the Foundation, who for many years have encouraged interest in the conservation of the 6,000 acres of landscape for which they are responsible. Sympathetic farming practices have been combined with support for the establishment of Kingley Vale National Nature Reserve (north-west of Chichester), the Weald and Downland Open Air Museum (see page 89) and the recording and monitoring of the archaeology and ecology of the estate.

THE SOUTH DOWNS are particularly rich in round barrows such as those on Treyford Hill. In the area between Butser Hill and Chantry Post there are at least 80 of these monuments on the Downs and on the sandstone ridge to the north. Plotting their locations on a map illustrates the fact that they occur on high ground and were presumably intended to be seen from considerable distances. When first constructed, the downland barrows would have stood out in the landscape as striking mounds of white chalk, their sides probably reinforced with basketwork or timber revetment.

Round barrows are associated with the Bronze Age period (about 2000 to 500BC in Britain) and they are often referred to as burial mounds. True, a lot of them contained burials, and the fact that many barrows now have a depression in the centre indicates the enthusiasm with which early antiquarians dug into them to see what they could find. But many barrows appear never to have contained human remains and their function may have been as much to define the boundaries of communities as to venerate the illustrious dead.

Many parish boundaries on the South Downs are marked by barrows and other prehistoric earthworks, suggesting that the definition of tribal or community territories has very ancient origins.

ROUTE DIRECTIONS

1. From Linch Down the Way runs through open land to Didling Hill, from which there are good views south and south-west to Chichester.

2. The Way then enters woodland, following the security fencing erected around the grounds of Monkton House, the house on the West Dean Estate formerly occupied by Edward James. There are peacocks in the grounds and you may be able to hear their cries.

3. In the wood the route turns sharply south-west to pass by the series of five large barrows known as the Devil's Jumps. The entrance is easy to miss, particularly if it is raining and you are preoccupied with staying on your feet.

4. At a major junction of paths in the wood on Phillisdown, the Way turns sharply right and heads off in a north-westerly direction towards Buriton Farm. Instead of turning right, thirsty travellers should continue straight on to the Royal Oak at Hooksay.

A RECTANGULAR Iron Age fort was built on Beacon Hill and at one time a windmill stood on the summit. This was one of the many sites on the Downs which were chosen as the location of signal fires, traditionally used to warn of the possibility of invasion and to mobilise the militia. The system was used, with predictably haphazard results, during the Spanish wars of the 16th century and the period of threatened French invasion in the early 19th century.

More modern methods of communication are illustrated by the location of Telegraph House, south of Beacon Hill. A series of telegraph towers between London and Portsmouth enabled communications to be sent by semaphore from the Admiralty to the Fleet in Portsmouth in the mid-19th century. Telegraph Hill, near Midhurst, is the next link in the chain, 5½ miles (10km) to the north-west of Beacon Hill.

From Beacon Hill there are panoramic views north to Combe Hill above Rake, north-west to Black Down, and on to Hindhead and the Surrey Hills.

ROUTE DIRECTIONS

1. From Hooksay retrace your steps to Philliswood Down and turn left, following the Way signs through woodland and then across open farmland to the access road to the remote Buriton Farm (which is nowhere near Buriton).

2. Turn left and them almost immediately right and climb up to Pen Hill at about 670ft (200m). At the junction of four paths you have a choice: either to follow the Way south towards Telegraph House and then north-west to rejoin the escarpment at Bramshott Bottom, or to remain on the ridge and climb over Beacon Hill, at 793ft (242m) quite a formidable obstacle.

3. Whichever route is chosen, the paths come together at Bramshott Bottom and from here it is a reasonably gently ascent over Harting Down to the county council car park on Harting Hill.

N

THE DOWNS here overlook the villages of South, West and East Harting. The principal settlement in the parish is South Harting, a charming village with a broad main street, a gabled Victorian school and several good pubs. The naturalist Gilbert White, of Selborne fame, lived here for a while, as did Anthony Trollope, the famous Victorian novelist. In addition, H. G. Wells has associations with the area, his mother having been housekeeper at nearby Uppark House, and the sculptor Eric Gill was responsible for the war memorial in the parish churchyard. The church of St Mary and St Gabriel is a large building which dominates the village. Although the general effect is largely 14th-century, the nave walls may be older and the roof, which was renewed after a fire in 1576, has been described (by Pevsner) as 'an anthology of Elizabethan carpentry'.

Uppark, a late-17th-century mansion ½ mile (1km) south of the escarpment, was one of the best country houses in Sussex until a disastrous fire in 1989 destroyed the whole of the interior. The National Trust, who owns the house and the adjoining estate, and also Harting Down, has embarked on an ambitious restoration programme under the direction of The Conservation Practice of Midhurst. Fortunately most of the contents of the house and even samples of wallpapers, curtains and other decorative fabrics were rescued as the fire spread from the roof. The debris from the fire is being carefully studied by archaeologists and, already, far more is known about the history of the house than before the fire. The roof is now back on the building but restoration work will continue for a number of years. Opening times are variable as a consequence.

UPPARK HOUSE

ROUTE DIRECTIONS

1. From Harting Down there are good views north over the Rother valley, with the foreground dominated by the village of South Harting and the green spire of its parish church.

Uppark House is still undergoing extensive and painstaking restoration by the National Trust after being severely damaged by fire in 1989

2. From the car park on Harting Hill, cross the main Chichester to Petersfield road with care and pick up the South Downs Way on the other side, slightly to the north.

3. Follow the track, negotiate the Emsworth to South Harting road, and the Way leads you to a trig point on Hemner Hill at 485ft (145m).

BURITON was the traditional end, or beginning, of the South Downs Way until it was officially extended to Winchester in 1989. The village, just in Hampshire, has a substantial parish church, a good village inn and attractive houses grouped round a pond. The houses include flint-and-sandstone cottages and a mainly 18th-century manor house which at one time belonged to the father of Edward Gibbon, author of *The Decline and Fall of the Roman Empire*.

The extension of the South Downs Way to Winchester was generally welcomed as clearly the Sussex and East Hampshire Downs have much in common and together constitute what most people think of as the South Downs, even if there are significant differences in the topography of the two areas. In addition, attractive as Buriton is, the ancient city of Winchester is a more fitting end to a great walk than a relatively insignificant and inaccessible downland village.

The extension to Winchester, however, has by no means been completed. There are still arguments about the route in certain places, there is incomplete bridleway continuity so riders need to check the position with the county council before attempting the route and the signing leaves a great deal to be desired. Typically, signing will send the walker off in great style from a main road or other access point and then abandon him to his own devices. To walk the Hampshire section of the South Downs Way successfully, it is essential to go armed with this guide and a detailed map on which you have marked the definitive route: you cannot depend on the presence of signposts to show you the way.

ROUTE DIRECTIONS

1. Continue along a farm track for a further mile or so (2km) to the county boundary at Hundred Acres.

2. The route then descends gently towards Sunwood Farm, the first habitation in Hampshire, and makes its way through the farm in a generally westerly direction.

3. When the road turns south at a lodge to Ditcham Park School go straight ahead towards Coulters Dean Farm, again aiming westwards.

4. Shortly before the farm a footpath descends the scarp on a diagonal line towards the village of Buriton where there is post office, shops and two pubs.

HUNDRED ACRES

Buriton, the first — or last — village to be reached in Hampshire

The edge of Petersfield, with its boating lake, can be seen beyond Buriton

THE PARK takes its name from the woodlands on War Down planted by the Forestry Commission in 1953 to mark the coronation of the present Queen. Trees were originally planted on War Down in 1928, shortly after the Forestry Commission was set up in order to ensure that Britain was not entirely dependent on imported timber. The country park was established jointly by the Forestry Commission and Hampshire County Council and, although it is mainly woodland, the 1,400 acres of the park include Butser Hill, to the west of the A3 and accessible from the centre by a tunnel under the road.

Queen Elizabeth country park is the jewel in the crown of the county council's active countryside management service and is intensively used for recreation: hang gliding, fun runs, grass skiing, pony trekking and orienteering are all encouraged, concentrating these activities in an area where they can be accommodated and managed. There is still plenty of room for family walks, picnics, barbecues and generally enjoying the countryside.

Four miles (7km) away to the north is the country town of Petersfield, 'capital' of East Hampshire. A pleasant town with a railway station, some interesting old houses in Sheep Street, Dragon Street and College Street and the famous Petersfield Bookshop, Petersfield is spoiled by the constant roar of traffic on the A3. Thankfully, the construction of a new bypass is now under way.

ROUTE DIRECTIONS

1. From Coulters Dean Farm continue westwards. In the vicinity of Dean Barn, cross over the London to Portsmouth railway line, which runs in a tunnel through the Downs.

2. A little further on the Way crosses a road (Kiln Lane) and you may turn right here to Buriton. The Way then bears left and takes a south-westerly direction across War Down towards the Queen Elizabeth country park centre.

3. There are many paths in the country park and opportunities to go wrong. If in doubt, always take the path which descends downhill.

WILDLIFE OF THE SOUTH DOWNS

Adonis blues are only found on chalk grassland where its food plant, horseshoe vetch, grows. The poor female is actually brown, but both sexes can be identified by the black-and-white bar markings on the edges of the wings. The caterpillar has yellow stripes and, as with several other blues, is 'milked' by ants

NATURE has conspired to complement the attractive South Downs landscape with a diverse array of wildlife. Perhaps best known for their colourful flowers and butterflies, these rolling chalk hills have much to offer anyone with an interest in the countryside and there is something to see throughout the year.

The appearance of the South Downs was largely created by man: native woodlands were felled and a close-cropped grass sward encouraged by the nibblings of generations of sheep and rabbits. Sadly, much of this flower-rich habitat has gone and been replaced by cereal fields. However, along the length of the Way there are still plenty of opportunities to marvel at remnant areas of downland and many of the typical flowers, insects and birds thrive along the downland hedgerows and paths. The flowering season begins early on the Downs. In April and May look for cowslips and primroses growing in the grassland. Hedgerow shrubs also burst into flower in the spring: sprays of white blackthorn flowers appear earliest in the season, to be followed in May by those of hawthorn. It is not until July and August that the full glory of the downland flowers is revealed. Knapweeds, harebell, wild carrot, yellow-wort and several species of orchids are just some of the more attractive species to look out for. Marjoram and thyme announce themselves not only by their flowers but also with their delightful fragrance. Autumn brings its own delights with a colourful crop of berries: black bryony, hawthorn, spindle and wayfaring tree are perhaps the most striking. With the wealth of downland flowers it is not surprising that insect life is also abundant, with butterflies being most in evidence. Keep an eye open for blue butterflies in particular: chalkhill and adonis blues are almost exclusively found on downland because their caterpillar's foodplant — horseshoe vetch — only thrives on chalky soil. Marbled whites, easily recognised by their black-and-white wing markings, are also common and can frequently be seen feeding on knapweed flowers. Alongside them you may also see burnet moths — day-flying species — which have burnished black and red markings. As you walk along the Downs, skylarks are invariably constant companions. Their delightful song is delivered in flight and at almost any time of year.

Harebells, commonest of the bellflower family, flourish in dry grassland. Their leaves are narrow and stalkless, and occasionally the flowers may be white or pale pink. The Scots call them bluebells

A tangle of poisonous black bryony berries such as this is a familiar sight along the hedgerows of the South Downs in autumn. Black bryony is the only British member of the yam family — a group of tropical plants with edible tubers — and takes its name from the colour of the tubers which are also poisonous unless boiled. White bryony (all parts of which are poisonous) similarly takes its name from the colour of its roots

Most other downland birds tend only to sing in the spring at the start of the breeding season. One of the most characteristic songsters is the yellowhammer whose song is sometimes rendered as 'a little bit of bread and no cheese'. Look for this colourful bird perched on fence posts and hawthorn branches. Related to the yellowhammer is the corn bunting. They prefer open fields and sing their rasping song from fence posts around the field margins. Just to the west of the Seven Sisters lies the mouth of the River Cuckmere. Here, visitors can find all the typical chalk downland flowers, insects and birds alongside small patches of saltmarsh where coastal birds to be seen include black-headed gulls, terns, redshanks, ringed plovers and dunlins. In addition, the Cuckmere valley is renowned as a place to observe bird migration. It is normally one of the first places that newly arrived swallows and wheatears are seen each year.

Yellowhammers feed their young almost exclusively on green caterpillars and insects, both parents often gathering food together away from the nesting territory. The male has much brighter colouring than the female, and the plumage of juveniles may have very little yellow at all

Easily identifiable by its bright red legs, the redshank favours estuarine salt marshes such as Cuckmere Haven, wet meadows and rough pastureland. Its noisy alarm call has given it the nickname 'sentinel of the marshes'

Butser to Exton

12 miles (19km)

This stretch involves the ascent of Butser Hill, the highest point on the South Downs, and the opportunity to explore Old Winchester Hill, with the prospect of a welcome at The Shoe Inn, Exton, at the end of the day. The high valley between War Down and Butser Hill, through which the modern A3 runs, represents an important topographical boundary which affects the character of the rest of the walk. All the way from Eastbourne the route has followed the single, bold escarpment of the South Downs, but this feature terminates at War Down. From now on, the walk does not follow a single ridge but a chain of high points in a gentler and more rolling landscape. This contrast provides a foil to the rest of the walk and a very satisfactory conclusion to the South Downs Way.

Butser Hill, which forms part of Queen Elizabeth country park, retains a considerable amount of prehistoric settlement

THE BUTSER Archaeological Farm is in Chalton Lane (the first turning left off the A3 as you head south from the country park) and is well worth a visit. It provides a vivid illustration of how our ancestors may have lived and worked on the Downs.

ROUTE DIRECTIONS

1. Arrive eventually at the country park centre near the busy (and noisy) A3. There is a café and lavatories at the centre (the first public loos since Whiteways Lodge, near Arundel!).

2. From the car park, follow the signs (in Hampshire, sometimes the words 'South Downs Way', sometimes an acorn, sometimes nothing) under the A3 and climb up Butser Hill.

3. On Butser Hill there is a round refreshment kiosk and public lavatories with a thatched roof, designed to resemble an Iron Age hut.

4. Turn left down the road and, following the South Downs Way signs, take the second turning right down a lane with a sign saying 'Unsuitable for Motors'. Follow the lane to Tegdown Hill.

1. From Tegdown Hill the Way runs over Hyden Hill to meet the East Meon to Horndean road near a trig point at 660ft (197m). Horndean, which lies a few miles to the south, is the home of Gales Ales, the local brewery which supplies excellent beer to pubs in East Hampshire and the Chichester area.

2. Cross the road and walk past the main gate to HMS *Mercury*, the Royal Navy's School of Maritime Operations, Communication and Navigation. The road follows the security fence and swings round to the left where it runs through the naval establishment between high fences with gates guarded by armed young men and women in battledress. Regrettably, the days are gone when walkers could pop into the NAAFI for a cup of tea and a bar of chocolate!

3. On the right, a section of an Iron Age boundary earthwork has been preserved as part of the grounds of a country house called Leydene, which was here before the arrival of HMS *Mercury*.

4. The South Downs Way turns sharp right just before the sports field. Walk past a bungalow named Spion Kop and climb up to a trig point at 780ft (234m) on Wether Down.

HMS *MERCURY* is engaged on matters of vital national importance but, from the walker's point of view, its presence in the middle of a long-distance path is unwelcome. No doubt the Ministry of Defence feels much the same about walkers! The other, and more important, disadvantage of the official route is that it avoids East Meon, one of the loveliest villages on the whole route. As will become clear, it is possible to detour into East Meon from Coombe Cross during the next section of the walk, but a more satisfactory approach would be to leave the South Downs Way by the car park at Butser Hill and descend the scarp slope to Ramsdean, from which a footpath runs west to the village of East Meon. From the village, take the road to Duncombe Farm and, shortly after the farm, turn right and follow a footpath to Henwood Down, where you rejoin the Way.

The buildings of HMS Mercury, *securely anchored, are named after naval heroes*

THE ATTRACTION of East Meon derives both from its situation and the way in which man has provided buildings which, individually and collectively, enhance and complement the natural setting. The village is situated at a point where the River Meon, one of Hampshire's famous chalk streams, squeezes between Park Hill to the north and Henwood Down and Small Down to the west and south. Park Hill, at 670ft (207m), is a dominant feature, providing a dramatic backdrop to the buildings of the village, with centre stage being taken by the parish church, its massive tower justifying East Meon's claim to dispute Alfriston's title as 'the cathedral of the Downs'. The River Meon flows along the main street of the village, with bridges providing access to the houses. There is a comfortable inn, The George, a post office and a shop.

William Cobbett, of *Rural Rides* fame, visited East Meon in November 1822. He was impressed: 'Here is a very fine valley, in nearly an elliptical form, sheltered by high hills sloping gradually from it: and not far from the middle of this valley there is a hill nearly in the form of a goblet-glass with the foot and stem broken off and turned upside down. And this is clapped down upon the level of the valley, just as you would put such goblet upon a table. The hill is lofty, partly covered with wood, and it gives an air of great singularity to the scene.'

ROUTE DIRECTIONS

1. From Wether Down follow the Way over Salt Hill to the tiny settlement of Coombe Cross. Travellers wishing to visit East Meon should turn right and follow the road into the village and then retrace their steps to rejoin the Way.

2. Continue north up Henwood Down towards Hen Wood. Just before the wood and before the hill begins to climb steeply, the route turns left into a field.

3. Walk down the field to a road, turn right and then left into Whitewood Farm, crossing a bridge over a tributary of the River Meon, which has been dammed here to create a landscape feature.

Sheep grazing, appropriately, on Wether Down: a wether is a castrated ram

Old Winchester Hill, including its hillfort, is a National Nature Reserve where many now uncommon downland species of butterfly can be found

OLD WINCHESTER HILL

N

NO-ONE KNOWS how Old Winchester Hill got its name: it is miles from Winchester and if any site has a claim to be the predecessor of the Saxon capital it is the hillfort on St Catherine's Hill, just east of the modern city. Whatever the origins of its name, Old Winchester Hill is crowned by the earthwork remains of a medium-sized hillfort built in the last 500 years BC and enclosing 14 acres within the rampart walls. The ramparts may originally have had a vertical outer face and would certainly have had a wooden palisade running along the top. There is a group of barrows to the west of the site and the parish boundary still runs along their centre line. The hillfort has never been excavated, although most of the barrows have been dug into and their contents, if any, removed. The hilltop was acquired by the predecessors of English Nature (the Nature Conservancy Council) and declared a National Nature Reserve in 1954. It contains fine examples of various chalk habitats, open grassland, scrub — including juniper — and beech woodlands.

ROUTE DIRECTIONS

1. From Whitewood Farm climb diagonally up the eastern slope of Old Winchester Hill, looking back over to the radio masts on Wether Down and Butser Hill.

2. Turn left when you meet the road and begin to walk south and west round Old Winchester Hill. There are a number of points of entry to the hilltop from the road and you can take any one you choose. The important thing is to make your way to the trig point on the top of the hill (660ft (197m)), from which there are panoramic views south to the coastline between Chichester Harbour and Southampton Water.

3. From the viewpoint the Way runs west and then north, past a sign urging walkers to be careful of ground-nesting birds. The route descends into a valley where the chalk of the uplands gives way to clay with flints and the land is in arable production.

4. Don't walk as far as Peake Farm but turn west to follow a stream bed which runs down towards Exton. If the main path is impassable in winter, there are alternatives on either bank and even stepping stones to cross the trackbed when the stream is in full flood.

Exton, one of the string of appealing villages in the Meon valley

ROUTE DIRECTIONS

1. Press on westwards. The ground can be very wet here and the route crosses the River Meon by means of a white-railed footbridge.

2. After crossing the river, the South Downs Way meets the busy A32 West Meon to Fareham road. Cross carefully and head down a lane immediately opposite which brings you to the village of Exton.

3. From Exton church walk along the curved main street and turn right at a bridleway sign. The path divides after a while and, if you are riding, bear left to join the road from Exton to Lomer Farm. If you are walking, take the right fork and climb diagonally up a large field to join the road near the summit of Beacon Hill.

WITH THE TEST and the Itchen, the Meon makes up the great trio of famous Hampshire chalk streams renowned for their clarity and, hence, their abundance of fish, particularly brown trout. The Meon rises from a principal spring at South Farm below Wether Down and flows due north to East Meon, where it changes direction and flows north-west and west to West Meon. Here it changes course again to flow south-west to Warnford, where, finally, it decides to head due south for the sea, passing through Exton and Titchfield *en route*. The Meon eventually enters the sea at Titchfield Haven, a relatively unspoiled estuary on the coast between Portsmouth and Southampton managed by the county council as a nature reserve. Izaak Walton, the 17th-century author of *The Compleat Angler*, fished the Meon, using East Meon as his base, and spent his last years at Warnford.

The curious early course of the immature River Meon reflects the nature of the landscape through which it passes, with the chalk hills of the main range of the South Downs combining with free-standing eminences like Park Hill and Barrow Hill. It is in this harmonious variety between the scattered hills and the valleys carrying the pure chalk stream of the young river that so much of the charm of the Meon valley lies. William Cobbett referred to the area as 'a high, hard, dry, fox-hunting country' and the great H. J. Massingham, author of *English Downland*, declared that he would rather spend his last days in the Meon valley than anywhere else in England.

Rudyard Kipling moved to the East Sussex village of Burwash from Rottingdean in 1902 and remained there until he died in 1936. His home, Batemans, is now owned by the National Trust. Burwash was an important centre of the iron industry — as recalled in the village sign — so it is not surprising to learn that Batemans was built for a local ironmaster

ART, MUSIC AND LITERATURE

UP UNTIL the First World War the South Downs were relatively unknown outside Sussex and Hampshire and the people who lived there were too busy struggling to make ends meet to be too concerned with the finer things of life. Early tourists venturing on to the Downs from the rapidly developing resort of Brighton were unimpressed: Dr Johnson remarked that the place was so desolate that, if a man had a mind to hang himself in desperation, he would be hard pressed to find a tree to fix the rope on!

The coming of the railways and increasing standards of living, however, resulted in the Downs being discovered by literary and artistic types who previously had had little connection with the area. A good example was the poet Edward Thomas, who moved to Hampshire with his wife and family from Kent in 1906 so that their children could attend Bedales School, near Petersfield. Other literary incomers included Rudyard Kipling and Hilaire Belloc. Both born abroad, they adopted Sussex as their home – Kipling lived near Burwash and Belloc at Shipley – and praised it in verse with the passion of the outsider. Particularly memorable are Belloc's *The South Country* and Kipling's *Sussex*.

This popularisation of the South Downs encouraged more visitors and settlers, some of them of an artistic bent. Thus, artistic and literary communities developed in a number of previously unremarkable rural locations. Charleston Farm, near West Firle, was occupied by the artists Duncan Grant and Vanessa and Clive Bell, while Virginia Woolf had a house at Rodmell. Frank Brangwyn and Eric Gill worked at Ditchling, John Galsworthy lived at Bury and D.H. Lawrence wrote *The Rainbow* at Greatham, near Pulborough.

Composers drawn to the South Downs included the nomadic Edward Elgar, who produced his famous Cello

Leading Bloomsbury artists Vanessa Bell, Clive Bell and Duncan Grant lived as a *ménage à trois* at Charleston Farmhouse, and it was Vanessa and Duncan, with their son Quentin (Bell), who painted the murals inside the church at nearby Berwick. The paintings were commissioned during the Second World War by the Bishop of Chichester. Local landmarks can be identified in some of the scenes

Concerto when he was living near Fittleworth, Arnold Bax, who spent his last days at Storrington, and Hubert Parry, who lived in a Norman Shaw house at Rustington. The composer who drew most on the South Downs for inspiration was John Ireland, who lived in a converted windmill near Washington and is buried at Shipley. His Piano Concerto and Amberley *Wildbrooks Suite* are both evocative of a part of Sussex he grew to love.

There is also a considerable amount of local literature relating to the South Downs, much of it of some merit. Outstanding is W. H. Hudson's *Nature in Downland*. but also of interest is the work of Richard Jefferies, Barclay Wills, Arthur Beckett, Tickner Edwardes, A. A. Evans, E. V. Lucas and S. M. P. Mais.

Music of an international standard was brought to Sussex in the 1930s when John Christie built an opera house in the grounds of his home near the village of Glynde. Since then, Glyndebourne has become synonymous with top-class opera and the social cachet attached to the extended intervals during which champagne and elaborate picnics are consumed is considerable

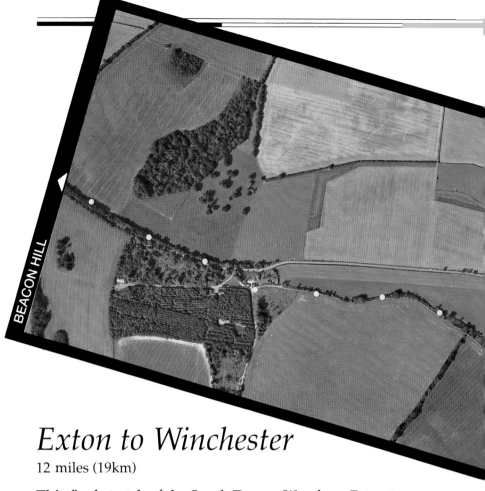

Exton to Winchester

12 miles (19km)

This final stretch of the South Downs Way from Exton to Winchester is largely through open, rolling countryside with long views to all points of the compass. The route climbs out of the Meon valley to Beacon Hill (670ft, 201m) and heads off north-west to Gander Down. The Way then changes direction to recross the road at Cheesefoot Head before dropping down through Chilcombe to the valley of the River Itchen and the city of Winchester. There is a pub at Milbarrow Down, about 3 miles (6km) from Exton, and all facilities, including accommodation, shops and bus and rail connections, in Winchester.

THE LUMPY nature of the ground at Lomer and the presence of stinging nettles are sure signs that the area has been disturbed and that, under the soil, the traces of an earlier settlement can be found. There were many reasons why villages were abandoned — crop failure, enclosure, plague — and sites like Lomer indicate the mobility of human settlement over time.

Hampshire's famous trout stream, the Meon, crosses the Way at Exton

118

ROUTE DIRECTIONS

1. On the approach to Beacon Hill there are good views east over the Meon valley and it is possible to follow the erratic course of the river as it changes direction at West Meon and Warnford — the latter can be identified by its church tower.

2. Follow the road north-west from Beacon Hill, diverting to cut off a corner by walking along a footpath through the field to the right. Take the road ahead of you and fork left at a footpath sign to follow the track past the site of the medieval village of Lomer and Lomer Farm.

3. Find your way through the farm buildings in a generally north-westerly direction and follow the path to Wind Farm on the road between Warnford and the A272. Turn left and walk along the road towards Millbarrow Down.

Formal design and informal planting are an effective combination in the gardens of Hinton Ampner. Its beautiful setting provides good views

ABOUT 1½ miles (2½km) north-east of Holdings Farm and an easy walk by footpaths is the village of Cheriton, where there are pubs, a post office and a shop. It is also possible to pick up a bus from Cheriton to Winchester or Petersfield. Near Cheriton Wood, east of the village, is the site of an important Civil War battle fought here in 1644 when the Parliamentary army under Sir William Waller defeated the King's army, led by Sir Ralph Hopton, thus checking the Royalists' advance to London from the south-west. Out of some 20,000 men who took part in the battle, over 2,000 lost their lives.

The River Itchen rises near Cheriton and also close by is the National Trust's Hinton Ampner House; both house and gardens can be visited. 'Hinton' means village on high ground and 'ampner' is a corruption of almoner, the medieval manor being owned by the Bishop of Winchester and associated with the office of almoner to St Swithin's Priory.

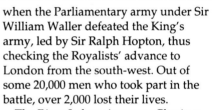

ROUTE DIRECTIONS

Between Lomer Farm and Wind Farm the Wayfarer's Walk joins the South Downs Way. The Wayfarer's Walk, devised and waymarked by the county council, runs the length of Hampshire from Emsworth on the coast to Inkpen Beacon near Newbury. Details from the county council in Winchester.

1. The pub on Millbarrow Down is now called Milburys, although it appears on some maps under its old name of The Fox and Hounds. Standing on high ground, the pub was supplied with water by means of a deep well shaft. Buckets were raised with the aid of a large wheel which accommodated not a donkey, as at Saddlescombe, but a man (or more likely a woman), it being the task of a servant to tread the wheel in order to draw up water. The wheel is inside the pub and, in exchange for a contribution to charity, the bar staff will give travellers an ice cube to drop down the shaft — the time taken for the cube to hit water giving some idea of its depth.

2. Go north from the pub and bear first left. Follow Holdings Lane for about 1½ miles (2½km) north-west to Holdings Farm on the A272 Petersfield to Winchester road.

NORTH OF CHERITON is the village of Tichborne and the small and attractive town of Alresford, just to the west of which the River Itchen, flowing south to north at this point, is joined by its tributary, the Alre. The Itchen then flows west past Itchen Stoke, Itchen Abbas, Ovington, Avington and Easton to Abbots Worthy, where it turns south to run through the valley in which Winchester is situated, between Twyford Down to the east and Teg Down and Compton Down to the west.

Tichborne is perhaps best known as the result of the famous 19th-century law suit involving the 'Tichborne Claimant', a fraud perpetrated by an obscure Australian who claimed to be Roger Tichborne, the heir to the Tichborne Estate, who was thought to have been lost at sea.

Alresford is a charming town with several pubs, restaurants and tea rooms and is a good base for exploring the South Downs Way in East Hampshire. The original village is known as Old Alresford, and New Alresford was a new town founded in 1200 by Bishop Godfrey de Lucy of Winchester, who dammed the Alre, created a reservoir, canalised the Itchen above Winchester and built a series of mills to harness the power of the water for industrial purposes. The Mid Hants Steam Railway, known as the Watercress Line, runs between Alresford and Alton and during the summer is very popular.

ROUTE DIRECTIONS

1. Cross the A272 carefully and walk up the farm track straight opposite. When the track meets a bridleway at a T-junction, turn right and follow the path along the edge of the field towards the wood. Unless you want to go to Cheriton, don't go into the wood, but turn sharp left and follow the path north-west towards the power line which runs over Gander Down.

2. Ahead, on the hilltop, is the woodland on Cheesefoot Head, pronounced Chessfoot locally. Walk towards the woodland, past Ganderdown Farm and under the power line. Cross a minor road which runs over Gander Down from Alresford to the A272 at 340ft (102m) and take the track immediately opposite ascending the hill to the north-east of Cheesefoot Head.

White-painted Tichborne House lies just east of the village, a delightfully unspoilt place with a pub, a church and thatched cottages

②

①

WILLIAM COBBETT had an encounter with a gipsy girl near here on one of his journeys. The girl he met was tall, dark and with beautiful features. He stopped his horse and asked her to tell him his fortune. 'She answered in the negative, giving me a look at the same time that seemed to say it was too late, and that if I had been thirty years younger she might have seen a little of what she could do with me.' Cobbett, for all his earnest interest in agriculture and political economy, was not indifferent to a pretty face. He visited Avington, north of here, from time to time and on one visit was critical of the turnips on the Duke of Chandos' estate. However, 'I was in some measure compensated for the bad turnips by the sight of the duke's turnip hoers, about a dozen females, amongst whom there were several pretty girls, and they were as merry as larks'.

The village and house at Avington, according to Cobbett, are 'both of them beautifully situated, amidst fine and lofty trees, fine meadows and streams of clear water'. Little has changed today and Avington Park is a perfect 18th-century period piece. Opening times are limited.

ROUTE DIRECTIONS

1. Continue along the track to a crossroads by a collection of barns, one of them painted green. Turn left and walk uphill towards Cheesefoot Head, with Temple valley below you to the left.

2. As you approach the woodland, pause to enjoy the wide, open views of the north over the Itchen valley. The path continues just inside the wood, which is mainly beech, and emerges eventually at the A272 Winchester to Petersfield road, just north-west of the trig point at 579ft (176m) on the summit of Cheesefoot Head.

3. Cross the road carefully and follow a South Downs Way sign into the field straight opposite.

4. A short distance into the field you come to a crossroads. Following the Way sign, turn right here. If you go straight on, you can make your way into Winchester over Deacon Hill and the north-eastern slopes of Twyford Down, but this is a less satisfactory approach than the official route.

5. The South Downs Way heads north-west for Winchester past a barrow on the left to Telegraph Hill (540ft (162m)). There is another earthwork on the summit of the hill, from which there are panoramic views over Winchester.

Crop circles near Cheesefoot Head: it would be nice to think they're not man-made

THE VIEWS in all directions from Telegraph Hill are spectacular. In addition to the western prospect to Winchester, you can see south over Fawley Down to the oil refineries at Fawley on Southampton Water. One of the Roman roads to the city of *Venta*, from which Winchester originated, approached the city from this direction, along the line of the modern road from Morestead to Owlesbury.

Chilcomb is a well-heeled, horsey sort of a place with an unspoiled early Norman parish church dedicated to St Andrew and a good VR posting-box let into a wall. John Washington, a relative of George Washington, the first American President, was rector here from 1803 to 1812 and is buried in Winchester Cathedral. It is hard to imagine that the duties attached to the post were unduly onerous.

For many years the authorities have been struggling to find a solution to Winchester's traffic problems and, in particular, to the overloading of the M3/A33 bypass. The current proposal is to tunnel through Twyford Down, although this plan is opposed by many people on conservation grounds.

ROUTE DIRECTIONS

1. Descend the hill to Chilcomb, following the track and bearing right at an ash tree. Don't take the path which goes straight on: it leads into the Ministry of Defence's Chilcomb Range and a red flag flying indicates that firing is taking place.

2. Follow the road through Chilcomb and, where the houses end and the road turns sharp left, take a footpath across a big field towards a bridge with grey metal parapet railings which carries the South Downs Way over the busy M3 Winchester bypass.

A detail of Chilcomb, the last village on the South Downs Way before reaching Winchester

N

WINCHESTER is the county town of Hampshire and the ancient capital of England, to the extent to which that expression can be applied to the fluid political arrangements of the times. Originally a centre developed by the Belgic people at a convenient crossing point on the River Itchen, the settlement was Romanised as *Venta Belgarum* and was one of the largest towns of Roman Britain. The Saxons settled here, built a church and elevated Winchester to the status of chief town of the Kingdom of Wessex, which Alfred successfully defended against the Danes.

With the arrival of the Normans, work started on the construction of the cathedral, which was begun in 1079. The building was eventually completed in more or less its present form by Bishop William of Wykeham in 1404. Wykeham also founded Winchester College (motto: Manners Makyth Man) and New College, Oxford. The bones of St Swithin, a notable 9th-century bishop, were enshrined in the cathedral which became an important pilgrimage

destination in the Middle Ages. The cathedral was built on a great raft of logs laid on the marshland by the river and, by 1900, the building was sinking. A diver, William Walker, worked for five years in the dark removing the rotten foundations so that they could be replaced by concrete.

ROUTE DIRECTIONS

1. For the time being riders must end their journey at Chilcomb, but walkers may press on across the footbridge, past All Saints' parish church, and down Petersfield Road and East Hill to Chesil Street.

2. Cross into Wharf Hill, where you may wish to look in at the friendly Black Boy for refreshment and to celebrate your arrival in Winchester.

3. From The Black Boy, find your way by the river to the bridge and the City Mill, which dates from 1743. Now owned by the National Trust, the mill is open to the public during the summer. Part of the property is leased to the YHA and houses a youth hostel.

4. Turn left and make your way to King Alfred's statue in the Broadway, the natural conclusion to the walk. The statue was erected in 1901 to mark the 1000th anniversary of Alfred's death.

Winchester Cathedral, the final and fitting destination for all those who have walked the South Downs Way from Eastbourne . . . or the beginning

Index

Index to places along the South
Downs Way

Adur River	58, 62
Alciston	32
Alfriston	22, 33
Alresford	122
Amberley	76
Amberley Mount	77
Amberley Wildbrooks	76
Angmering	36
Annington Hill	63, 65
Arun River	76
Arundel	72, 78, 81
Ashcombe Plantation	45, 49
Avington	124
Baily's Hill	16
Balmer Down	45
Barnsfarm Hill	68
Beachy Head	12, 16
Beachy Head youth hostel	27
Beacon Hill (Hants)	119
Beacon Hill (W Sussex)	96
Beddingham Hill	36, 37, 38
Beeding Hill	60
Bepton	92
Bignor	36, 81
Bignor Hill	83
Birling Gap	14
Blackcap	49
Blackpatch Hill	72
Bopeep Bostal	32
Bostal Hill	32
Botolphs	63
Bourne Hill	28
Bramber	61, 62
Bramber Beeches	65
Bramshott Bottom	96
Brass Point	16
Brighton	57
Bullock Down	12
Buriton	100, 103
Burpham	60, 75
Burpham Hill	75
Burton Down	82
Bury Hill	78, 81
Butser Archaeological Farm	107
Butser Hill	106
Chalk Pits Museum	78
Chanctonbury Ring	36, 66
Chantry Post	72
Charleston Farmhouse	32
Charleston Manor	20
Cheesefoot Head	124
Cheriton	121
Cheriton Wood	121
Chilcomb	126
Cissbury Ring	72
Clayton	54
Clayton Hill	56
Cocking	89
Cocking Down	92
Combe Hill	28
Coombe Cross	110
Cowdray Estate	88
Cow Gap	12
Cricketing Bottom	40
Crowlink Estate	16
Crown Tegleaze	84
Cuckmere Haven	14, 19
Cuckmere River	18
Devil's Dyke	56, 59
Devil's Jumps	94
Didling	92
Didling Hill	95
Ditchling	50
Ditchling Beacon	51, 52
Downs Link	63
Drusillas Zoo	23
Duncton Hill	82, 84
Dyke Hill	57
Eartham	83
Eastbourne	10, 27, 36
East Dean	14, 27
East Meon	108, 110
Edburton Hill	52, 59
Exceat	19
Exton	114
Falmer	42
Firle	32, 34
Firle Beacon	34
Firle Place	34
Fishbourne	36
Flagstaff Brow	16
Flagstaff Point	16
Flat Hill	16
Foxhole	19
Friston Forest	20
Frog Firle youth hostel	20
Fulking escarpment	59
Gander Down	122
Glynde	34
Glynde Place	34
Goodwood Estate	88
Graffham	87
Graffham Down	87
Gumber Bothy	83
Harrow Hill	49, 72
Harting Down	96, 98
Harting Hill	96, 99
Hartings, The	98
Haven Brow	16, 19
Hemner Hill	99
Henwood Down	108, 110
Heyshott	86
Heyshott Down	88
Highden Hill	68
Hinton Ampner	121
HMS *Mercury*	108

Holt Brow   31
Hooksway   95
Horndean   108
Houghton Bridge   60, 77, 78
Hundred Acres   100
Hyden Hill   108

Ilford   42
Itchen River   122
Itford Hill   36, 38

Jack and Jill windmills   54
Jevington   28

Keymer   52
Kingley Vale   93
Kingston Hill   42
Kingston-near-Lewes   42
Kithurst Hill   73

Lavant River   87
Levin Down   88
Lewes   39, 44
Linch Down   92
Litlington   20
Littleton Down   84
Lomer   118
Long Man of Wilmington   31
Lower Standean   52
Lullington church   23
Lullington Heath   31

Meon River   110, 115, 119
Mid Hants Steam Railway   122
Millbarrow Down   121
Monk's House   40
Mount Caburn   34
Mount Harry   49

Newtimber Hill   56

Old Winchester Hill   113
Ouse River   32, 36, 38

Parham House   75
Park Hill   110
Patcham youth hostel   57
Peacehaven   40
Pen Hill   96
Perry Hill   75
Petersfield   103
Pevensey Bay   27
Philliswood Down   94
Piddinghoe   38
Plumpton   50
Plumpton Plain   49
Pyecombe   55

Queen Elizabeth country park   103

Rackham Hill   75, 77
Ramsdean   108
Rock   66
Rodmell   40
Rother River   86
Rough Brow   16
Rowdell   68

Saddlescombe   56
Salt Hill   110
Seaford College   85
Seven Sisters   14, 16
Short Brow   16
Singleton   89
Slindon Estate   83
Small Down   110
Southease   38, 40
Springhead Hill   75
Stane Street   83
Steyning   65
Steyning Bowl   65
Steyning Round Hill   65
Storrington   73
Streat   50
Streat Hill   49
Summer Down   57
Swanborough   42

Tegdown Hill   107
Telegraph Hill   96, 126
Telscombe   40
Telscombe youth hostel   40
Tichbourne   122
Treyford Hill   94
Truleigh Hill   56, 59, 60
Truleigh Hill youth hostel   61
Trundle, The   87
Twyford Down   126

Uppark House   98

War Down   103
Warningcamp youth hostel   75
Warren Hill   26
Washington   68
Watercress Line   122
Wayfarer's Walk   121
Weald and Downland Open Air
  Museum   89
Went Hill   16
Wepham Down   75
Westburton Hill   81
West Dean Estate   93
Westdean   20
West Hill   56
Wether Down   110
Whitebread Hole   13
Wilmington   31
Winchester   128
Windover Hill   31
Wiston Estate   66
Woolavington Down   85
Worthing   68

Useful Organisations

The following bodies may be contacted at the addresses given for any further information required.

Countryside Commission, John Dower House, Crescent Place, Cheltenham, Gloucestershire GL50 3RA

Forestry Commission, 231 Corstorphine Road, Edinburgh EH12 7AT

National Trust, 36 Queen Anne's Gate, London SW1H 9AS

English Nature, Northminster House, Peterborough, Cambridgeshire PE1 1UA

English Heritage, Spur 17 Govenment Buildings, Hawkenbury, Tunbridge Wells, Kent TN2 5AQ

Long Distance Walkers' Association, 9 Tainters Brook, Hempsted Fields, Uckfield, East Sussex TN22 1UQ

Ramblers' Association, 1/5 Wandsworth Road, London SW8 2LJ

Youth Hostels Association, Trevelyan House, 8 St Stephens Hill, St Albans, Herts AL1 2DY

South East England Tourist Board (Sussex), 1 Warwick Park, Tunbridge Wells, Kent TN2 5TA

Southern Tourist Board (Hampshire), The Old Town Hall, Leigh Road, Eastleigh, Hampshire SO5 4DE

The Society of Sussex Downsmen, 93 Church Road, Hove, East Sussex BN3 2BA

Page 1:   Springhead Hill
Pages 2 and 3:   Burton Down; The Long Man of Wilmington
Pages 8 and 9:   Tichborne House; Cocking Down; background picture, Edburton Hill